Distant Melodies

DISTANT MELODIES

Music in Search of Home

EDWARD DUSINBERRE

The University of Chicago Press

The University of Chicago Press, Chicago 60637
For more information, contact the
University of Chicago Press, 1427 E. 60th St., Chicago, IL 60637.
Published 2022
Printed in the United States of America

31 30 29 28 27 26 25 24 23 22   1 2 3 4 5

ISBN-13: 978-0-226-82343-0 (cloth)
ISBN-13: 978-0-226-82344-7 (e-book)
DOI: https://doi.org/10.7208/chicago/9780226823447.001.0001

First published by Faber & Faber Ltd, 2022.

Library of Congress Cataloging-in-Publication Data

Names: Dusinberre, Edward, 1968– author.
Title: Distant melodies : music in search of home / Edward Dusinberre.
Description: Chicago : The University of Chicago Press, 2022. | Includes
    bibliographical references and index.
Identifiers: LCCN 2022009736 | ISBN 9780226823430 (cloth) | ISBN
    9780226823447 (ebook)
Subjects: LCSH: Dusinberre, Edward, 1968– | Violinists—Biography. |
    Musicians—Travel. | Takács Quartet. | Dvořák, Antonín, 1841–1904. |
    Elgar, Edward, 1857–1934. | Bartók, Béla, 1881–1945. | Britten, Benjamin,
    1913–1976. | String quartet.
Classification: LCC ML418.D97 A3 2022 | DDC 787.2092 [B]—dc23
LC record available at https://lccn.loc.gov/2022009736

♾ This paper meets the requirements of ANSI/NISO Z39.48-1992
(Permanence of Paper).

To my parents, Juliet and Bill

Contents

Members of the Takács Quartet

Gábor Takács-Nagy, first violinist, founding member, 1975–92

Károly Schranz, second violinist, founding member, 1975–2018

Gábor Ormai, violist, founding member, 1975–94

András Fejér, cellist, founding member, 1975–present

Edward Dusinberre, first violinist, 1993–present

Roger Tapping, violist, 1995–2005

Geraldine Walther, violist, 2005–2020

Harumi Rhodes, second violinist, 2018–present

Richard O'Neill, violist, 2020–present

PART ONE

Here and Elsewhere

To play the violin demands a delicate juggling of proximity and distance. Resting between chin and collarbone, my instrument responds to the smallest variations of bow speed and placement. Too needly: I move the bow faster and further from the bridge. Too diffuse: I move the bow nearer the bridge, slowing it down to create a more direct sound. The tonal possibilities that I discover within my violin shape my expectations: whether I imagine the musical character as constricted or soaring, inviting or remote, when I make a sound that conveys that specific mood, I am briefly content. Later, when I return to the same melody, I call upon my muscular and auditory memory, adjusting vibrato, bow speed and contact point, searching for that same effect.

The first musical experiences that I remember occurred at home in Leamington Spa. At one end of our L-shaped living room was the mahogany Welbeck upright piano that my mother played, accompanying my first efforts on the violin. When we played simple violin duets together, she encouraged me to choose an energetic bow-stroke to make a rhythm sound livelier. At the other end of the room, the gramophone's loudspeakers were at ear level as I sat on the floor playing with my toys nearby. When

Jacqueline du Pré played the robust chords at the beginning of Elgar's Cello Concerto, it was as if she was in the room with me.

While the immediacy of these sounds grabbed my attention initially, as I grew older my mother introduced me to other concepts. At the beginning of a slow movement, she showed me that the first note I played need not be an explicit beginning: by approaching the string more smoothly with my bow, I could create the effect of joining music already in the air. Similarly, at the end of a slow movement, she encouraged me to taper my last note instead of just stopping the bow, blurring the moment at which the melody faded into silence. In this way, she explained, an audience could continue to hear the music even after I had stopped playing it. I did not realise it at the time, but this was my first introduction to music's capacity to evoke a time or space beyond my immediate surroundings.

As first violinist of the Takács Quartet for nearly three decades, I have become intrigued by the different ways in which music can be both immediate and distant. On stage, I and my quartet colleagues sit as close to each other as is practical without risking collisions between bows and scrolls, relying on such proximity to play in tune and synchronise rhythms, to blend or differentiate our sounds from one another. If I cannot hear a viola melody or cello rhythm clearly, I lack the confidence to play my own part. At the same time, if I feel too crowded by the sounds around me, I am forced to play louder than I would like. Some early pictures of string quartets show the players seated across from each other in a closed circle, like four players at a bridge table. As chamber music has moved from smaller salons to larger halls, the circle has opened out. Across our group we maintain a wide semi-circle, preferring that the first violin and viola, sitting on the outside, do not obscure the second violin and cello. However intimate the interactions between players on stage, music is now expected to reach audiences across larger distances.

The Turkish author Elif Shafak once described the experience of self-imposed exile: while grappling with disorienting physical separation and the unfamiliarity of language and culture, it is hard to throw off a sense of not being fully present.[1] In the years that have passed since I moved from England to the USA, initially to study in New York in 1990, and then to join the Takács, I have become more aware of music's capacity to both bridge and accentuate distance. When a melody triggers a vivid memory it may both offer a connection to the past and illuminate how far one has travelled. This book explores ideas of home, displacement and return in the lives and chamber music of four composers whose works I began playing early in my musical life: Antonín Dvořák, Edward Elgar, Béla Bartók and Benjamin Britten.

A few years ago I sometimes found myself ground down by the demands of life in a string quartet, struggling to retain a sense of joy in my music-making as the Takács performed a wide array of music, including the difficult quartets of Britten and Bartók. At the other end of the spectrum, Dvořák's 'American' Quartet was reduced in my mind to an effective concert piece that could be polished up with little rehearsal, an antidote to more challenging fare. But during this period I was drawn again to the stories and music of these three composers who all spent time living in America, trying to reconcile their new surroundings with nostalgia for their homelands. Dvořák arrived in New York from Prague in October 1892 to take up a position as director of the National Conservatory. Britten and Bartók came to America from London and Budapest respectively following the emergence of Hitler and Nazism. I began to pay more attention to surprising departures and homecomings within their lives and music, and especially to those pivotal moments where melodies return transformed, the music moving in a surprising direction, throwing one off kilter.

The Takács Quartet has evolved into a very different group from the four young Hungarians who began playing together in 1975 as students at the Franz Liszt Academy in Budapest. Only cellist András Fejér remains from the original ensemble. Changes of second violinist and violist in recent years have made me aware of how a piece of music may both reinforce roots and cross borders, its capacity to both anchor and untether its players and listeners. While my first book, *Beethoven for a Later*

Age, delved into the inner workings of a string quartet, this one charts the progress of the Takács during a period of change and subsequently as we emerge from the COVID-19 pandemic.

A scene from Tom Stoppard's *The Invention of Love* has remained with me ever since I saw the play at the National Theatre during its opening run. Recently deceased poet and Classics scholar A. E. Housman is helped from Charon's boat by a young man who is studying Classics at Oxford, just as Housman did many years before. The young man describes a hill near his home in Worcestershire that he and his siblings named Mount Pisgah, from where they looked out to a kind of a Promised Land – in fact the Clee Hills in Shropshire. Housman recognises his undergraduate self: 'Well, this is an unexpected development. Where can we sit down before philosophy finds us out. I'm not as young as I was. Whereas you, of course, are.'[2] The two versions of Housman sit chatting on a bench by the River Styx.

More practical than a trip down the River Styx, music offers a space where younger and older versions of oneself can coexist. On the copy of Dvořák's Sonatina for violin and piano that my mother passed on to me, she had written her maiden name in black biro pen, 'Juliet Stainer'. Underneath, scribbled in pencil, my own signature was an early and unconvincing experiment in joined-up writing. Dvořák composed the piece in New York for his children Antonín and Otilie who gave its first private performance in New York in December 1893. I first played the piece when I was nine years old, my mother's amused protestations at a difficult semiquaver figuration in the last movement of the piano part adding greatly to my enjoyment of the project. Nearly two decades later, in July 1993, I again associated Dvořák with the exhilaration of new experiences.

My first professional assignment in the Takács was to perform the 'American' Quartet, composed in Spillville, Iowa. I was grateful to channel excessive adrenalin through its lively rhythms and catchy melodies. But a piece of music only becomes a lifelong companion when new elements emerge to resonate with different stages of life. The longer I have lived away from England, the more I have been drawn to Dvořák's music written both in the USA and when he returned to Bohemia, music in which he attempted to reconcile the distance between his new surroundings and his homeland. Different aspects have emerged to commingle with the music and memories of my youth.

A significant feature of Bartók's compositional technique is his treatment of recapitulation: often the so-called return of a primary melody is an opportunity for disorienting transformation. Bartók finished his sixth and final quartet in November 1939, around the same time that he made the anguished decision to leave Hungary and move to New York. He returned repeatedly to the sad opening melody that begins the work, eventually revising his initial plan to end the piece with fast music by instead allowing the slow melody to take over the entire last movement. I associate the piece with my first trip back to England to perform with the Takács in November 1993. During my first concert at Wigmore Hall I was too caught up in the giddy excitement of my new life to inhabit fully the sense of loss that permeates the work. Nearly thirty years later my perspective has been changed, in part by returning to Budapest where we performed the piece in the same hall where Bartók gave his last concert in Hungary, and also by visiting Bartók's last home in Hungary, where he composed the piece. During the last troubled years of his life in the USA, Bartók mourned his homeland: in his music at least he could control the narrative of return.

Melodies encounter their previous selves in various ways, either within the same piece or between pieces written years apart. I first played Benjamin Britten's 'Playful Pizzicato' and 'Frolicsome Finale' from his *Simple Symphony* as a teenager, its humour and lively dialogue linked now in my memory to the camaraderie of playing in a youth orchestra. Britten completed the piece in 1934 when he was twenty years old and in his final year at the Royal College of Music, revisiting musical themes from piano pieces and songs he had composed between the ages of nine and twelve. Seven years later, during the summer of 1941, he composed his String Quartet no. 1

under unusual circumstances in California, discovering a new connection to his homeland that changed the course of his life. My own experience of this piece was changed by being grounded in Boulder during the COVID-19 pandemic: when travel is forbidden, the ways in which a piece of music transcends distance become more palpable. In 1975, at the age of sixty-two, Britten returned to past melodies again, this time revisiting his opera *Death in Venice* to quote some of its themes in the last movement of his String Quartet no. 3, the last major work he composed before he died. To rehearse and play the piece at home in Boulder, Colorado, was to experience Britten's music differently from during my teenage years.

Throughout his life Elgar linked his music to specific places and to ideas of home. Ever since I first heard du Pré's recording of the Cello Concerto, Elgar's music has connected me to home and my musical heritage. A few years ago I began to play an Elgar work with which I had no previous associations. As I learned more about Dvořák, Bartók and Britten's American experiences, Elgar's Piano Quintet and the landscapes that inspired it provided another way to explore the ways in which a piece of music may affirm or alter one's sense of home.

The regretful opening phrase from the 'Enigma' Variations heard over my car radio still takes me back to my grandparents' cottage, floorboards creaking as Grandpa descends the stairs, his pocked bald head barely avoiding a wooden beam. Silencing the standing clock, he switches on the radio and sits down next to me, opening a miniature score between us. We begin to listen to a live concert broadcast on BBC Radio 3. Grandpa nods appreciatively at the first shift from minor to major key, pointing out the surprising twists that unfold as Elgar transforms his opening melody.

My mother's father, grandson of the homonymous Victorian composer John Stainer, was head of music at Shrewsbury School before becoming registrar of the Royal College of Music in 1959. After his retirement in 1976, my grandparents moved back to Shropshire, buying a small cottage fifteen miles west of Shrewsbury. In the local community they built a rich musical life. My grandfather played organ in Worthen Church and conducted a local amateur orchestra, one of several in which my gran played the oboe. Grandpa also enjoyed playing the viola in both chamber groups and local orchestras.

Mondaytown was the name of my grandparents' cottage and of a tiny hamlet consisting of a farmhouse and two cottages, accessible by a lane that gradually ascended from the village of Aston Rogers, close to the Welsh border. After I opened the gate that marked the beginning of the Mondaytown farmer's land, the car bumped over potholes, its underside scraping along tall grasses that grew down the middle of the lane. Only after the lane curved right and left could I see beyond the farmyard to the rusty white gate at the bottom of my grandparents' garden.

Grandpa played daily the Bechstein grand piano that took up nearly half the living room. Snippets of Schubert, Beethoven and Chopin floated through an open window while my younger brother Martin and I played outside among overgrown hedges and fruit-laden trees. We invented a hybrid football-golf game using tree trunks in place of holes, trying to avoid yet relishing the moment when the ball landed on the curved driveway and began to roll down between the damson trees, gathering speed before thwacking into the gate. When my gran, Thea, practised oboe in the kitchen, the sound carried to the adjoining paddock where we played cricket on a pitch that Grandpa had fashioned by cutting earth out of the hill and redistributing it to minimise the slope. I imagine that Gran conveyed beautifully the wistful intricacies of Benjamin Britten's *Six Metamorphoses after Ovid* for solo oboe, but at the time I was more alert to a loud exclamation against the vagaries of an unruly reed, followed by a slammed door – both hopeful indicators that she might shortly appear on the garden terrace to offer us a piece of her unbeatable fruit cake.

I practised the violin in Grandpa's study off the main room, an ambitious teenager eager for an audience. When I thought there might be people eavesdropping, I would jump to a flashy passage in a concerto. It was a dubious ploy, my parents and grandparents easily able to discern the difference between focused practice and showing off. Grandpa by contrast was grateful for an audience with whom to share his delight in a dramatic change of mood or a surprising chord change. That he did not crave praise is perhaps one reason why he continued to enjoy playing the piano until the end of his life. A photograph taken a few days before he died on 9 January 2014, six days before his ninety-ninth birthday, shows him seated at the Bechstein, leaning forward towards his music, his face creased in an expectant smile. As elements of his life faded around him, music provided a way for him to retain the delight of clarity and recognition.

After I moved to New York in August 1990 to study at the Juilliard School, the memory of my grandparents' melodies heard from the garden acquired an unsettling, melancholy flavour: fragments that had vanished in the air, replaced by the chatter of swallows whose descendants perhaps still return each summer to nest under the eaves. In my first letter home from New York I offered an upbeat account of Orientation Activities in Central Park, failing to mention that I had returned to my grimy furnace of a bedroom at the West Side YMCA and vomited from heatstroke. Omitted also from my report were the feelings of homesickness that hit me like one of the trucks that blared down Columbus Avenue, a disorientation further increased by the first encounter with my new violin teacher, Dorothy DeLay: 'Now let's see . . . are you Nicholas Milton from Australia?'

Nonetheless, my transition to life in America at the age of twenty-one had little in common with those international students anxiously dependent on sponsors to support their visa applications. As a result of my father being a US citizen, several months before I left for New York I had descended the steps of the embassy in London with my first US passport, observed by a partisan pigeon who offered farewell felicitations by shitting on my head. The following August I explained to a customs official at New York's John F. Kennedy International Airport that the large number of traveller's cheques in my possession were necessary to pay my tuition fees. 'What's Juilliard?' She cut off my nervous reply: 'I'm just messing with you – of course I know what it is. Have a great year!'

During my first semester in New York I had not reckoned on the rude comments of my Juilliard peers about Elgar's music and ideas of Englishness, an early warning that clinging to notions of home could be a precarious activity. Following a painfully overblown interpretation of Elgar's First Symphony, the Juilliard Orchestra's English guest conductor exclaimed, 'Bravi, bravi' before wiping the patriotic fervour off his brow. One violinist added 'Marvellous' to his arsenal of rehearsal asides while another wrote off Elgar's music as 'repressed yet overwrought'. Scarcely in a tone of eager anticipation my stand partner observed, 'It's as if one of your royals is about to enter the room. Better than Vaughan Williams I guess, but Elgar doesn't exactly travel well.'

I pointed out that the First Symphony had been well received, performed eighty-two times during the year following its first performance in 1908. Admittedly, most of these concerts had taken place in England. I dreaded to think what my friends would do with the London *Times*'s later elucidation of the First Symphony's popularity: 'Enterprising commercialists even engaged orchestras to play it in their lounges and palm courts as an attraction to their winter sales of underwear.'[3]

The fourth floor of the Juilliard School was filled with airless practice rooms devoid of daylight, their dirty yellow carpets a repository for stains of uncertain origin. In this hub of the music school where practising alone for many hours each day cultivated self-absorption like mutating bacteria, I missed the Boxing Day gatherings that my uncle and aunt had hosted at their home in the Essex countryside, forty miles south of Cambridge. Between breathless and muddy football games, my cousins, brother and I joined our parents and grandparents to play chamber music. When we read through Elgar's *Serenade* for string orchestra my mother led the second violins, at one point turning around to remonstrate cheerfully with my father: 'Come on William, aren't you going to play?' But except for sporadic efforts, he preferred to let the violin rest on his chest as he savoured the sounds of activity around him. Above raucous laughter inspired by our occasional derailments, Grandpa, playing viola, shouted out bar numbers from where we resumed our efforts. The memory of such revelry was in sharp contrast to the awkward grimaces Juilliard violinists offered

during performance classes – a pre-emptive acknowledgement of errors in advance of feedback from our peers.

When I first played the *Serenade* I enjoyed the return
of musical themes from the first movement near the
end of the piece, a resolution more satisfying following
mishaps along the way. The *Serenade* was one of Elgar's
earliest published compositions, emerging from the
musical community in Worcester where he grew up. His
father William, a piano tuner, pianist and violinist, was
eager that his six children should become good enough
instrumentalists to participate in the local music scene.
In addition to learning the piano, from the age of seven
Elgar took violin lessons from the leader of the Worcester
Glee Club Orchestra. In the music room on the second
floor of the Crown Hotel on Broad Street the members
of the club explored a wide array of composers including
Handel, Mozart, Bellini and Rossini. At the age of twelve
Elgar joined the orchestra, one of several local organisa-
tions that enabled him to develop his craft as an arranger,
composer and conductor. In May 1888, when Elgar was
thirty years old, the Worcester Musical Union first performed his *Three Pieces* for string orchestra. Although
the manuscript has been lost, based on the movement
titles alone it was almost certainly an early version of the
Serenade. Throughout his life Elgar retained an affection
for this early work and the institutions that inspired it. In
1932, two years before his death, he revisited the Crown
to attend one of the Glee Club's last meetings.

When fellow Juilliard students made fun of Elgar, they did not mean to belittle the significance of such lifelong ties or of those convivial Boxing Day gatherings that had increased my eagerness to become a professional musician, but their comments touched a nerve. Nostalgia and sensitivity to criticisms of Elgar did not fit well with my self-perception as an adaptable traveller.

After I moved to Colorado, I began to worry that by being so tied to narrow ideas of Englishness, Elgar's music might indeed not travel well. In the opening scene of *A Hidden Portrait*, a BBC documentary about Elgar, the camera pans back from mottled grasses to reveal the conductor Sir Andrew Davis ascending a peak in the Malvern Hills. To the sombre accompaniment of the BBC Symphony Orchestra playing 'Nimrod' from the 'Enigma' Variations, Davis muses on Elgar and characteristics of the English:

> Our love of ceremony, a deeply passionate nature
> that no stiff upper lip can truly conceal, a wry sense
> of humour, a tendency to melancholy, pride in our
> achievements, and a profound attachment to our unique
> countryside. Elgar has it all.

Perhaps. But if the Olympics were to introduce a 'Melancholia' category, England might already face fierce competition in the heats. As for that lauded upper lip, such rigidity could just as well betray a lack of empathy as hide a reservoir of passion. Were the English really any more attached to the modestly contoured Malvern Hills than Coloradans to the dramatic vistas of the Continental Divide? In North America *nimrod*, far from meaning a hunter or warrior, was a term for an idiot. Hoping not to encounter the First Symphony in the underwear section of J. C. Penney's Boulder store, I began to avoid Elgar – his music, so I thought at the time, a regressive intrusion as I adjusted to the idea of settling in America.

My dual citizenship was an enviable privilege for a travelling musician. I liked being able to whip out my English passport throughout the countries in the European Union and yet be welcomed home by US customs officials whenever I passed through Dulles Airport outside Washington DC. Teaching and playing concerts at the Aspen Music Festival between 1998 and 2015, I often found myself in Aspen for Independence Day celebrations. At City Market in the centre of town, I cheekily offered 'Happy Fourth' greetings in my fruitiest English accent, before witnessing an extravagant firework display over the mountains. If I ever felt unmoored, it was in mid-air above Newfoundland, as the years passed since my departure from England, increasingly aware of a pattern of missed weddings, funerals and anniversary parties, of student friendships reduced to brief emails or hasty post-concert meals.

A few months after my Grandpa's death in 2014, I found a photograph and description of the cottage's living room posted online by the listing agent:

Lounge/Diner with parquet wood flooring, exposed ceiling beams, open brick fireplace and hearth oak mantle, seated bay window, staircase rising to the first floor, secondary front entrance door with porch and tiled steps.

In the photograph the room was empty: no one smiled expectantly at the music and there was no grandfather clock to be silenced. The Bechstein had been moved to storage. Less suspicious of nostalgia than during my first years in Boulder, I could admit my attachment to the English countryside, more poignant now because I had never really said goodbye to Mondaytown. Having attempted to banish Elgar, I began to look to his music again as a way to retain a sense of home, to counter the unnerving distance I sometimes felt from both my adoptive and home countries.

Elgar's Hills

In May 2016 I travelled to Symonds Yat, a small village in the Wye Valley, for the Takács Quartet's annual CD recording project for Hyperion Records. At the end of the first day's sessions, I walked from the Old Court Hotel past the now deserted primary school, turning left again at a roundabout and continuing on a road parallel to a noisy, dual carriageway section of the A40. Escaping the traffic, I climbed up a steep staircase enclosed on both sides by hedges, before emerging through a gate into a field high above the village. On past visits I had enjoyed this vantage point, easily enough reached even after washing down a steak and chips with a pint of Stowford Press cider. Except for a few concerned sheep I had the field to myself. On the other side of the valley, Coppett Hill rose steeply above the River Wye, the ruins of Goodrich Castle barely visible in the encroaching dusk. During the Civil War the castle had been severely damaged in a violent conflict, besieged Royalists eventually capitulating in the intimidating presence of Roaring Meg, the Parliamentarian mortar.

Elgar linked this area to the genesis of a melody in his *Introduction and Allegro* for string quartet and string orchestra, composed in 1905. While walking in the hills, he was reminded of a previous experience by a fragment of song floating through the valley. Four years earlier from a cliff in Cardiganshire he had heard singing in the distance. Too far away to catch the whole melody, Elgar had been struck by the interval of a falling third. The 'Welsh tune', as Elgar not entirely convincingly labelled it, might have remained a discarded sketch except for the later Wye Valley experience. Elgar described the *Introduction and Allegro* as an appreciation of the border region where he made his home, using the falling third as a feature of a plaintive tune first played by a solo viola, accompanied by *pianissimo* strings.

One month before the United Kingdom referendum on whether or not to leave the European Union, Elgar was in the news. Harriet Baldwin, Conservative Member of Parliament for West Worcestershire, had outraged Leave supporters by manufacturing a photo opportunity with the famous bronze sculpture that looked down Church Street in Great Malvern. She had clad Elgar in a white T-shirt with red and blue lettering proclaiming 'I'M IN'. Next to Elgar, Baldwin wore a complementary blue T-shirt. With doleful facial expression and unyielding arms that forced the shirt awkwardly up Elgar's torso, the obdurate mannequin did little to promote the Remain cause. It stood about as much chance of swaying Brexiters as Leicester City supporters would of converting rival fans by singing 'WE HATE NOTTINGHAM FOREST!' to the tune of 'Land of Hope and Glory'.

Nonetheless, Elgar provides a good example of the importance of European connections for English musicians. In 1899, circumventing his initially dubious English publisher, the forty-two-year-old composer had sent the score of the 'Enigma' Variations to Hans Richter, at that time the conductor of the Vienna Philharmonic Orchestra, who came to England annually to conduct at the Birmingham Festival. Richter's enthusiasm for the work resulted in its first performance in London later that year. Although his support of Elgar's next major piece, *The Dream of Gerontius*, was not enough to coax a satisfactory first performance out of the choir at the Birmingham Festival in October 1900, nonetheless Otto Lessman, editor of the influential *Allgemeine musikalische Zeitung*, gave the work a glowing review. Lessman's fellow audience member Julius Buths, director of music for the city of Düsseldorf, recognised the potential of *Gerontius* and began to translate Cardinal John Henry Newman's words into German. Buth's performances in Düsseldorf that December and in May 1901 were crucial in advancing the early reputation of the piece; its subsequent championing by Richard Strauss and other leading German musicians paved the way for its further acceptance in England.

Less disturbing to me than Baldwin's misguided electoral strategy were the laser tag games on offer at the purpose-built battleground of Wye Valley Warfare, situated opposite my hotel in Symonds Yat. Here participants could benefit from updates to the cumbersome Civil War technology of Roaring Meg by choosing Predator or M9 laser weapons to complete two missions united by a common premise: 'European Government has broken down; armed militia, terrorists and bandits are in control.'[1] In Mission Alpha one could set Europe ablaze as a secret agent. Mission Bravo offered a longer-term project in which one could help the locals to seek, disrupt and destroy the insurgents. To recover from such strenuous efforts one could decompress at the adjacent Butterfly Zoo or among the statues of a twelve-hole 'Roman ruin fantasy' miniature golf course. On previous visits I had found it easy enough to dismiss Wye Valley Warfare as a fantasy, a dissonant element in an otherwise harmonious landscape, but in this period of divisive debate its disturbance of my favourite view from above the village troubled me. 'Yat' is an Old English word for gate, this part of the valley historically an important trading link over the River Wye. But trading links were now in jeopardy while increasing pollution endangered the river's ecosystem. The armed militia and insurgents of Wye Valley Warfare seemed like a fanciful distraction from the challenges facing the country.

A few days later I plummeted downhill from my hotel in Upper Wyche, thirty miles north-east of Symonds Yat, through a dense copse on a path that Elgar possibly walked more than a century before, to visit the graveyard in Little Malvern where Elgar and his wife Alice were buried. As I located their graves, a woman wearing a broad-rimmed beige sunhat emerged from behind St Wulstan's Catholic Church, carrying what looked like a picnic hamper but on closer view turned out to be a basket full of gardening tools.

'Good morning. I see that you've found it!'

'Thanks for the clear signs.'

'That's how the Elgar Society likes it, especially important as we welcome visitors from all over the world. Last week a Japanese gentleman was here, dressed up in a suit and tie. He knelt down beside the grave and wept – how remarkable for someone from so far away to be so moved by Elgar's music!'

For Alice's funeral on 10 April 1920, Elgar asked his friend violinist Billy Reed to assemble a string quartet. During the service the group played the slow movement of Elgar's String Quartet, one of Alice's favourite pieces. Elgar's description of the site was posted on a nearby information board: 'The place she chose long years ago is too sweet – the blossoms are white all around and the illimitable plain, with all the hills and churches in the distance which were hers from childhood, looks just the same – inscrutable and unchanging.' The blossoms remained but in the intervening years a row of poplar trees had been planted below the grave, obscuring the view: only by craning over a fence into the adjacent field could I see the mosaic of irregularly shaped fields that gave way to another range of hills in the distance – the placid agricultural scene less majestic than Elgar's illimitable plain suggested.

A published novelist who spoke German, Italian, French and Spanish, in 1899 Alice Roberts had married the son of a Catholic piano tuner eight years younger than herself, to the dismay of her Anglican family. Sacrificing her own literary ambitions and even ultimately her own health, Alice became an efficient business manager and an indispensable support for her demanding husband, who suffered from a variety of physical and emotional ailments. That the Malverns held so many memories of Alice perhaps accounted for Elgar's description of her grave site as being 'too sweet'. Fleeing the area shortly after the funeral, he visited his sister Pollie at her home in the Worcestershire village of Stoke Prior, the surroundings there less painfully evocative.

The woman gestured to the pristine flower bed in front of the grave. 'I've looked after the grave for nineteen years. The slow movement of the First Symphony, the end of the Cello Concerto, *The Dream of Gerontius* – those pieces make it all worthwhile.' She looked up with a slight smile. 'Even if he could be a bit of a poser at times. Growing up nearby, for so many years not feeling accepted in London, he was rarely happy, a bit too bothered what everyone thought of him. Even a knighthood didn't entirely remove his insecurity.'

In a setting more likely to inspire bland eulogies I was

surprised by her nuanced verdict – the implication that Elgar's output was uneven, his personality not always appealing. That she remarked upon the Japanese visitor's grief paradoxically suggested an awareness of the limits of Elgar's reach – at Bach's or Beethoven's grave such an outpouring by someone 'from so far away' would not have been worthy of comment.

The volunteer walked down the path back towards the church, placed her basket next to another gravestone and began to pull out weeds. Compared with the report she had given me of the grieving pilgrim, I was embarrassed by my more detached response. I could blame it partly on the lack of effort invested in my journey – an exhausting journey from Tokyo perhaps more conducive to emotional outpourings than a short trip on the 5.15 p.m. commuter service from Birmingham New Street. But my role as a violinist, sometimes expected to provide suitable music at weddings and funerals, had also influenced how I reacted to such occasions and settings. While attending a funeral no one wanted to be subjected to a snivelling violinist, tremulous bowing arm unable to produce a steady sound. At the Cambridge Crematorium I once played Bach's Sarabande from the D minor Partita – a suitably stark accompaniment as curtains drew around the coffin of a close family friend. My cool facade was a little too convincing. 'How thoughtful of the undertaker to supply a violinist,' a relative remarked, perhaps concluding that this was how I always earned my living on a Friday afternoon.

As I left the graveyard I mumbled goodbye to the dedicated volunteer – it seemed unlikely that she would be reporting my undemonstrative demeanour to the next visitor. Before I began to ascend the steep path towards the ridge that led to the Worcestershire Beacon, I passed a white cottage festooned with hanging baskets and the words 'As recommended on thebestofmalvernhills' painted in blue on a side wall. The promise of a wicker-tabled coffee shop offering slabs of coffee and walnut cake to fatigued tourists was dashed by a small wrought iron sign above the front door: 'Andrew Phillips Funeral Services'. A sudden demise while retracing my steps would at least be met with unparalleled service.

Later that day I sat devouring a piece of cake at a roadside café beneath the British Camp, a man-made earthworks that dates back to the Iron Age. For his cantata *Caractacus*, Elgar drew upon the legend of a British chieftain apparently associated with the British Camp who staged a last-ditch battle here against the Romans. In fact Elgar's librettist H. A. Acworth was aware of doubts concerning the exact location of this battle: Caractacus had the strategic advantage of a river in front of him, and fought at a site in line with the River Severn, more likely at Caer Caradoc in Shropshire.

As a young child Elgar had sat by the side of the River Severn with a notebook trying to capture the sound of the reeds. He linked a passage in *The Dream of Gerontius* with trees swaying in the wind and the opening of his

Piano Quintet with a group of dead trees struck by lightning near Fittleworth in Sussex. When friend and violinist Billy Reed visited the composer during his last illness in 1934, Elgar hesitantly sang the opening tune of the Cello Concerto before telling Reed not to be frightened if, while walking on the Malvern Hills, he heard the same melody in the form of Elgar's ghostly presence floating through the air.

As I puffed to the top of the Worcestershire Beacon no such sonic apparitions disturbed my walk, Elgar's music as remote to me as Caractacus.

In Kazuo Ishiguro's story 'Malvern Hills', Tilo and Sonja, a married couple on holiday from Switzerland who make a living performing traditional Swiss folk music, are drawn to a melody heard 'just in the wind at first'. They discover the narrator of the story, a young songwriter, sitting on a bench composing a song. He enjoys wandering on the less frequented Table and End hills, not so far from the village of Pershore where he had grown up. 'There I'd sometimes be lost in my thoughts for hours at a time without seeing a soul. It was like I was discovering the hills for the first time, and I could almost taste the ideas for new songs welling up in my mind.'[2]

Although Tilo and Sonja are happy to meet a fellow musician, tension between the couple escalates, in part caused by their differing reactions to the hills. Towards the end of the story the songwriter comes across Sonja sitting on the same bench alone. She has just argued with

Tilo, contradicting his assertion that the Malverns are 'even more wonderful' than Elgar's music. In Sonja's imagination 'Elgar's hills are majestic and mysterious. Here, this is just like a park.'[3] An understandable verdict from someone accustomed to the Swiss Alps.

Although the Malvern Hills and surrounding countryside were a crucial source of inspiration for Elgar, I too associated this music with a different landscape. Just sixty miles further north I used to look from my grandparents' kitchen window across the valley to the ridge of the Stiperstones, named for dramatic rock formations that included the Devil's Chair, ominous as it emerged from the morning mist. Even if Elgar tied his music to a specific landscape, it was equally valid for a listener to form his or her own associations. If Elgar had spent time rambling on the Stiperstones he might have been inspired by the legend of the Saxon earl whose ghost was rumoured to ride the ridge whenever England was threatened by invasion. *Caractacus* was however a more promising title for a choral work than *Wild Edric*.

My receptiveness to the Malverns was not aided by this evasive habit of seeking out the humour in a situation – Elgar's seemingly pompous description of the view from St Wulstan's. *The Wild Edric Oratorio*. Behind such jokes lay a greater avoidance. After Alice's death Elgar had escaped to Stoke Prior, a place unburdened by memories of her. In my case it was the Malverns where nostalgia could more easily be avoided. Recalling the view from

Mondaytown across the valley, I now understood Elgar's use of the term 'illimitable plain' to describe a landscape perhaps modest in reality, but more significant in terms of what it had come to represent.

Elgar's Retreat: What Remains

The perceived inconsistency of voice in Elgar's Piano Quintet is one reason for its relative lack of popularity, certainly by comparison with the Cello Concerto, composed around the same time. Perhaps part of the problem is a matter of expectations. Whenever I return to the Hyatt Hotel in Melbourne during a Takács Quartet tour, a TV welcome screen featuring the same pink London taxi that sits outside the hotel is accompanied by more stereotypically Elgarian music: a lush and lyrical section from the slow movement of his Second Symphony. For other hotel guests, perhaps this music seems suitably welcoming, but I find it a bizarre choice, the recycled excerpt too short, its relentless reiterations taking me back to my teenage years and an unfortunate incident during a National Youth Orchestra rehearsal of the piece when a wasp flew into the left trouser pocket of our conductor, Sir Charles Groves.

Elgar's more famous pieces are often employed more successfully to guide the mood of specific occasions. Particularly within the former colonies of the British Empire, 'Nimrod' from the 'Enigma' Variations is played for funerals or sombre events, such as the handing over of Hong Kong to China in 1997 (naturally during the

English rather than the Chinese part of the ceremony). The most extreme example of this phenomenon dates back to Elgar's trip to America in 1905 to accept an honorary degree from Yale University, the award facilitated by its professor of applied music, Samuel Sanford. 'Land of Hope and Glory' was played at the end of the ceremony and, after being similarly used by other universities, today remains a regular fixture at high school graduation ceremonies. Elgar dedicated his *Introduction and Allegro* (the piece inspired by melodies heard in Cardiganshire and the Wye Valley) to Sanford, who during a visit to England in 1904 had made Elgar a present of an upright Steinway piano, the same instrument on which he would later try out much of the musical material for his Piano Quintet.

The Piano Quintet is a work too unpredictable in mood to be of much use at public ceremonies. One of three late chamber works Elgar worked on while living in a cottage near the village of Fittleworth, Sussex, in 1919, it is characterised by a sinister atmosphere at its opening. The piano part begins with a serene plainsong chant undermined by a faster, spiky rhythm in the strings. As the movement unfolds jarring contrasts develop. After a section where the music moves forward urgently, the violins play a flirtatious melody above a quietly buoyant piano accompaniment, derived from but far removed in mood from the opening music. The exuberant music that follows seems to belong in a dance hall. The composer's friend, George Bernard Shaw, complimented Elgar on the atmospheric opening but took the composer to task for a fugal passage later in the first movement that regressed to the 'expected'. Elgar defended himself, saying that he intended the passage to be square before becoming 'wild again'. The quintet features odd juxtapositions of emotions and musical styles, resisting straightforward interpretation.

The fact that the Piano Quintet is not considered suitable fare for a graduation ceremony has increased my affection for it. In May 2017 when I travelled to Sussex to visit Brinkwells – the cottage that Alice Elgar first rented from artist Rex Vicat Cole in May 1917 – the spectre of the United Kingdom's withdrawal from the European Union loomed large. The sense of fracture that pervades the Piano Quintet suited my mood.

'Maybe the machine does not now like foreign cards.' A man with a German accent waved a ten-pound note in my direction outside Pulborough station. 'Can you pay with your card and I give you money?' After I purchased a train ticket for the flustered traveller, I walked under the railway bridge towards Fittleworth, unencumbered by my usual suitcase and eager to abandon my reliance on taxis to take me between airport, hotel and concert hall. I passed a young woman awaiting the bus, which according to my calculations could not possibly arrive for another forty-five minutes. Stinging nettles caressed my calves as

I stepped to one side to avoid fast oncoming cars, their fumes funnelled by hedges on either side of the road. After five minutes a green bus swished past me on the way to Fittleworth. I returned to the taxi dispatcher's office to the right of the station ticket hall. Half an hour later, I asked my taxi driver if he liked living in the area. 'Less crowded than Surrey. But we're getting busy here now too.' As we approached Fittleworth I explained that I was planning to visit Elgar's retreat. 'Oh, right. I didn't know that. "Land of Hope and Glory" – that's very English.'

In March 1918, at the age of sixty and after several years of deteriorating health, Elgar had undergone a tonsillectomy. Following the painful operation and a dispiriting period in a nursing home, Elgar returned to Brinkwells with Alice. When Alice rented the cottage, she envisioned Rex Vicat Cole's self-standing artist's studio in the garden as an ideal music room for her husband. After their arrival the Elgars and local handyman Mark Holden laid a wooden floor there. The same upright Steinway piano that Professor Sanford of Yale had given Elgar was retrieved from storage and delivered by train. From the station Farmer Alwyn, a neighbour who lived nearby at Spring Farm, carried it through the woods with his pony and cart.

When violinist Billy Reed visited the Elgars in August, Alwyn collected him from Pulborough station. Twenty years later Reed recalled his arrival in his memoir, *Elgar as I Knew Him*:

We jogged along through some wonderfully wooded country, along a road that twisted and turned continually, until at last we came to about half a mile of straight road rising up a fairly steep hill with chestnut plantations on each side. At the top of the hill, looming on the sky-line, was what at first sight I took to be a statue; but as we drew nearer it I saw it was a tall woodman leaning a little forward upon an axe with a very long handle. The picture was perfect and the pose magnificent. It was Sir Edward himself, who had come to the top of the hill to meet me, and placed himself there leaning on his axe and fitting in exactly with the surroundings.[1]

During Reed's visit the composer and violinist tried out several sections of a new violin sonata. After reaching a blank page they would ramble through the woods or go fishing in the nearby River Arun. Elgar was 'bubbling over with excitement' as he demonstrated his enthusiasm for woodworking. He enjoyed cutting, stripping and splitting chestnut poles, and clearing brushwood. With Reed's help he sawed through a barrel to create two tubs for Alice. Mark Holden was however unimpressed at Elgar's rough attempt to make a music stand for Reed. 'I am so glad you have come,' Alice said to Reed; 'it is lovely for him to have someone to play with.'[2]

Elgar exhibited a dangerous interest in chemistry, attempting to snuff out a wasp nest by pushing pieces of cotton wool soaked with cyanide of potassium into the entrance with his walking stick. Reed recalled that he and Elgar lit their pipes to await the return of the wasps:

> Hundreds soon littered the ground in front of the entrance, so that the new-comers had to scrape their bodies out of the way to get to the hole, adding their own bodies to the heap. Sometimes one would get only half a whiff of the poison: he would then dart about in the air, flying in a wild and erratic manner until he dropped dead in the road or returned to the hole for another sniff, which put an end to his career.[3]

At 4.30 the next morning Elgar awakened Reed and asked him to help dig out the remains of the nest, in case any children on their way to school should discover the carnage and be exposed to the poison. Reed plunged his spade into the earth but 'the din that arose, as of a million wasps all buzzing at once, sent us flying'.[4] Two pails of nearly boiling water administered by Mark Holden rescued the bumbling Londoners from their plight. Holden might have disagreed with Reed's description of the new summer tenant as blending in harmoniously with his surroundings. But such was Elgar's enthusiasm for the woods that in September he bought a small patch of woodland from the agent of the Stopham Estate.

My progress towards Brinkwells was slowed by several detours as I attempted to find the place at the top of the fairly steep hill where Elgar had stood waiting for Reed, who was aided by a printout of a map that Elgar had drawn. Of the many paths that approached Brinkwells, none provided more than a gentle incline. Perhaps a century of erosion and land management had minimised the contours. Or perhaps Reed's memory had inflated the drama of this landscape so entwined with the momentous time when he worked with Elgar on his last chamber works.

Despite respecting a number of 'KEEP OUT' signs affixed to gates and fences, courtesy of the Stopham Estate – the same landowner who had rented Brinkwells to Vicat Cole – I found myself in the middle of a clearing lined with small huts, perhaps an abandoned bowls club or a suitable arena to test acceleration in advance of the twelve-hour (nocturnal) lawnmower race that took place each year around Pulborough, organised by the British Lawn Mower Racing Association.

Turning right along a small road, I saw a small sign at the bottom of a tree. 'BRINKWELLS', written in gold lettering, was the only indication that I had come to the right place. Part of a thatched roof was visible behind high hedges. After walking down the driveway I passed a stone side wall of the cottage. Two small white-framed windows allowed the current residents to size up Elgar tourists as we walked past. Next to a parked car a spade was dug into newly spread earth. Across a field I could see the hills of the South Downs through the haze. A grazing cow cast me a lethargic glance. I had not arrived at Brinkwells with any plan beyond the hope of striking up a conversation with someone in the garden and perhaps being invited into the cottage. I continued through the garden, looking for the public path on which the Elgars would have walked up to Spring Farm. A dense patch of nettles blocked my way.

It was difficult to linger outside the cottage without intruding upon the privacy of its current occupants. Cole's studio was no longer at the same site: it had been moved to the nearby village of Bedham, and modified as the mainstay of a larger property. The concern of the current tenants to protect their own haven was understandable. This was no heritage site. No upright Steinway had been placed in a replica wooden-floored music studio nor manuscript paper and pencils placed on a desk, placid pony and cart on hand outside to give bored children a ride. I had no desire to look inside the cottage or find the relocated studio, where the current living arrangements might further erase my image of Elgar and Reed trying out new music or striding through the woods to fish in the River Arun, 'TROUT' happily scrawled in an ensuing diary entry. I walked back up the driveway and found a diagonal path through a field in the direction of the densely wooded area known as Flexham Park.

Elgar described the first movement of the Piano Quintet as 'ghostly stuff', referring in part to a local legend that had caught his imagination: some Spanish monks guilty of enacting impious rites had apparently been struck dead by lightning and transformed into burned trees. On 18 July 1918, Alice noted in her diary the arrival at Brinkwells of Algernon Blackwood, a writer of supernatural short stories and novels. After drinking tea, Elgar and Blackwood visited the trees. Two months later Alice linked the same spooky trees to the opening of the Piano Quintet. Billy Reed also heard the musical influence of the trees, describing the 'very gnarled and twisted branches stretching out in an eerie manner as if beckoning one to come nearer'.[5] The basis for the yarn about monks and their devilry was however dubious. There is no historical record of a monastery anywhere near Brinkwells, or of Spanish monks lurking in the area. The myth of the burned trees was probably the invention of the aptly named Blackwood. Another possible source of extra-musical associations for the quintet came in the form of *Strange Story*, an occult novel by Edward Bulwer-Lytton, that according to Alice 'seemed to sound through it too'.[6]

Although walking in the forest offered welcome shade, getting in among the particular group of dead trees associated with the dubious monks was a futile exercise, since they no longer existed. In fact Reed's description of the trees as being high up on a plateau pointed not to Flexham Park but to the nearby Bedham Copse: the trees were cut down many years ago, probably to make way for new roads. I walked back through the woods towards Fittleworth on the Serpent Trail, named not for the adders that Elgar frequently boasted of killing but for its many twists and turns. My appreciation of 'the most breathtaking countryside in the south-east' – according to the trail's official guide – was enhanced by frequent signs: 'STOPHAM ESTATE: Please keep dogs under close control'. On another gate nearer to the village, the words 'SMILE, YOU ARE ON CCTV' were highlighted by a bright yellow backdrop.

Plaques above the bar in Fittleworth's Swan Inn recorded the visits of Rudyard Kipling and Sir Hubert Parry; the latter had left a musical memento in a guest book in the form of his 'Song to the River'. In a 2015 news story for BBC South, presenter Ben Moore sought to reinforce the musical heritage of the inn as he walked through narrow corridors in which 'you can almost hear the strains of English music'. The inn boasted the additional distinction of having been an early meeting place for a humorous drinking club called the Ancient Order of Froth Blowers, their fundraising efforts for various charities in the 1920s and 1930s guided by the salubrious motto 'Lubrication in Moderation'.

I studied the map that Elgar had drawn for Billy Reed, the sort of work I might have offered as a homework assignment to illustrate a school report after visiting my grandparents' cottage, the use of explanatory labels an artistic technique perfected at primary school and persisting well into my later period. The map featured a stick-person self-portrait, both arms extended, one holding the leash of his new terrier Meg, the other a walking stick. Elgar painted his hat a vivid blue in contrast to the pallid colour of the River Arun. With a fisherman's optimism he filled the river with fish, although the one at the bottom of the map more closely resembled an upside-down penguin floating helplessly downstream. A black 'Smoke of WELCOME' came out of the chimney while the declaration 'WE HAVE COAL', highlighted in yellow and red, would have been welcome news to any guest to Brinkwells affected by reduced coal production during and after the First World War.

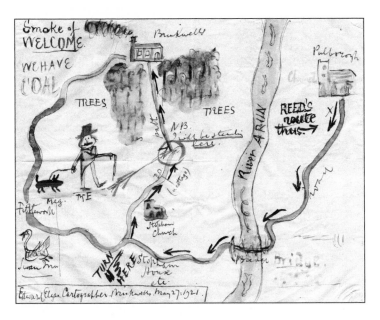

Only now did I notice the date on the inscription: 'Edward Elgar, Cartographer, May 27, 1921'. Full of detail to reassure the first-time visitor, the map did not after all date to Reed's first visit to Brinkwells in 1918. Drawn over a year after Alice's death from lung cancer on 7 April 1920 at the age of seventy-two, the map attempted to relive the sense of fun and adventure that had characterised Reed and Elgar's time together three summers previously.

When Elgar tried to buy the Brinkwells lease from Rex Vicat Cole, he hoped to maintain a shrine to Alice's memory in the form of a shelter that Mark Holden had built for her. Elgar forbade anyone to touch or use it, but a wren built a nest in the place where Elgar remembered Alice's head touching the roof-twigs. By April 1921 Elgar had found out that Vicat Cole and his wife planned to return to live at Brinkwells. With no possibility of a future there, Brinkwells provided scant consolation. In the Sussex haven Alice had created for her husband through her willingness to forego the greater comforts of life in London, her absence was all the more apparent.

The Elgar that I took away from Brinkwells was not the rejuvenated composer who in 1918 revelled in wood-work projects and for relaxation rushed down to the river to try out his latest fishing equipment, but the diminished man of three summers later, struggling to recapture Brinkwells through a map a child could have drawn. The past did not oblige, providing wrenching contrasts to his current state, threatening emotional equilibrium like the spectral melodies that return to undermine more energetic music. When Reed again brought his violin to Brinkwells, 'never was there anything new for me to play'.[7] 'Edward Elgar, Cartographer' was the inscription, both humorous and sad: Elgar continued to compose sporadically, but between 1921 and his death on 23 February 1934 he completed no works matching the scope of his Piano Quintet and Cello Concerto.

Near the end of Elgar's life, the efforts of Fred Gaisberg, an American musician who in 1898 had moved to England to become the first recording engineer for the Gramophone Company, enabled Elgar to revisit his earlier music and the places that had inspired it. Gaisberg arranged for the London Symphony Orchestra to record excerpts from *Caractacus* on 22 January 1934 at the Abbey Road studios. Elgar listened through loudspeakers set up in his bedroom at home in Worcester, providing feedback to the musicians through a microphone. At the end of the session he asked the orchestra to repeat a favourite section, 'Woodland Interlude', that had been inspired by the landscape of his childhood near the Malverns. With the help of his gramophone Elgar also recalled the woods near Brinkwells. Repeatedly he listened to a new recording of the Piano Quintet by Harriet Cohen and the Stratton Quartet. According to Billy Reed, the slow movement always moved its composer to tears. If revisiting Brinkwells had been a desolate experience, near the end of his life Elgar found another way to access memories of Alice, woodwork projects and walks among the trees.

*

Elgar's attempt to buy the Brinkwells lease and keep alive the memories of happier times was on my mind two years later when I finally returned to Shropshire. The day before my cousin and I visited my grandparents' graveyard, a Welsh farmer approached us on his tractor somewhere near the Offa's Dyke footpath, south of the Welsh village of Montgomery. 'Who's supposed to be reading that map?' he asked. I gestured to Dickon, several yards ahead of me as we crossed a field full of grazing sheep: after my navigational prowess had caused one detour, he had taken over the responsibility. 'Take it off him, he's got no bloody idea where he's going.' The farmer pointed to a stile behind us, his friendly tone spiced with satisfaction at correcting two English hikers striding ahead in the wrong direction.

Early the next morning the trees that towered above the graveyard at Worthen Church dampened extraneous sounds as effectively as they blocked views of the Stiperstones, the stomping grounds of Wild Edric long ago. We found the granite stone next to a hedge where hawthorns and hollies jostled for light:

THEOPHANIA STAINER

1st Feb. 1912 – 22nd Jan. 2006

JOHN RANALD STAINER

15th Feb. 1915 – 9th Jan. 2014

A precise reckoning of names and dates, softened by the addition of 'Our Dearest Thea' and 'Her Beloved Husband'.

So close to Mondaytown I felt the lack of music, the Bechstein piano long since moved to storage. I had missed Gran's funeral in 2006. In the middle of a Takács Quartet tour with the Hungarian folk music ensemble Muzsikás, I tried to imagine the sound of my uncle Gareth playing 'An Eriskay Love Lilt' at the graveside. A courageous choice to play the oboe on a chilly February day: with no opportunity to warm up he must have moistened his reed before the service, keeping the instrument warm under his jacket and surreptitiously blowing down it to clear any condensation before playing the first note. When Gareth began to learn the oboe as a child, Gran shared her own instrument with him. He used the same oboe, in his words, 'to play her to sleep, so to speak, as her body went to its last rest', choosing a folk song that they both played and a copy of the music passed down the generations from her own mother.

Now, as we stood by the grave, other music played in my head, an episode from Elgar's Piano Quintet where themes from the first movement return, disrupting the last movement. The viola is the first to suggest a departure with a flourish of faster notes – a gate opening onto a familiar but transformed scene. First the strings and then the piano create an ethereal shimmer of sound oscillating between the notes of one chord, the progression of harmonies suddenly arrested. The cello and viola are left alone quietly rocking between two notes. Then enters the opening music of the whole piece; the plainsong chant and undermining spiky rhythm are still recognisable, but modified to fit the triple metre of the last movement. Other fragments of music from the first movement recur. Mutes applied to the violins' bridges dampen the resonance and act like a sepia filter. The extended memory is a disruptive digression that recedes as quickly as it enters. As Matthew Riley puts it, such reminiscences might be nostalgic, but they are rarely therapeutic. 'The past may seem to offer truth and meaning, yet it is ultimately brushed aside, either eerily, brutally, perfunctorily, or with bitter irony.'[8] Although Elgar's most popular music – the *Serenade* for string orchestra, 'Land of Hope and Glory' or 'Nimrod' – could be appropriated to reflect one narrow facet of national identity, the Piano Quintet that risked such disruption spoke to the broader predicament of reconciling past and present, not specific to a particular country.

After Grandpa's death, the cottage had been bought at auction by the neighbouring farmer. In summer 2018, the year before our visit to the graveyard, a vigorous debate had intensified concerning a proposal presented by architects to the Shropshire County Council to erect a replacement dwelling there. The Responsible Officer recommended that planning permission be refused, objecting to the aesthetics of the plans for several reasons. The new house would be larger than the previous cottage and incongruous with nearby properties. Due to its prominent position, views from nearby footpaths would be adversely affected. Unimpressed with the proposed modern design, the officer recommended that the new dwelling be more traditional in its form and scale: local materials like stone and slate tiles should be used to build a house more resembling a converted barn or old cottage. Local residents expressed varied opinions, some concerned about the scale of the proposal, others praising the innovative design of the house that they felt complemented the local environment in an up-to-date way. Councillor Ed Potter argued that the proposal would replace a redundant cottage – according to him unused for many years – with a high-quality house of a modern design. After the architects worked hard to address the concerns, a committee of council members approved the application.

Recalling Elgar's despair during his final visit to Brinkwells, in that moment I lacked the courage to return to the site of the cottage where demolition was probably well under way. Underlying my choice was a desire not so much to brush the past aside as to find a way of preserving memories that was not so reliant on a particular place. Although I was at first distressed by Potter's description of the cottage where Grandpa had spent his last years as redundant, one suggestion in the council's report stood out, offering hope for the future.

Perhaps some fabric of the old building, such as the floor-boards, might be salvageable and used to repair other historic buildings.[9] The same floorboards that creaked as Grandpa walked along the landing to the top of the stairs could be reused like a musical theme, refashioned to shape the structure and story of a new piece. What remained from my childhood visits to Mondaytown were those elements capable of adaptation that could be taken elsewhere.

Several months after my trip to Shropshire, I travelled to Zurich where my brother Martin and his family had moved after he was appointed as professor of global history at the University of Zurich. As I sat on the terrace at the back of their apartment, I could see the Bechstein through the window. The piano had been retrieved from storage and transported by lorry from Shropshire; now it filled a corner of an airy, bright living room. Framed family photos and a vase of flowers stood on top of its lid. The music rack was crowded with music: beginners' piano and trumpet books, and the same collection of ver-nacular songs from which my brother and I sang, not only at Mondaytown but also in the houses in Leamington Spa and Cambridge where we grew up – anywhere with a piano and someone game enough to play it.

To the west the sun was setting over the ridge that connects the Uetliberg to Felsenegg, a ridge that my father used to walk along on Sunday afternoons in the early 1960s, a young American historian studying in

Zurich, before he settled in England. After my parents married, music became a way for my father to get to know his father-in-law. Before dinner he encouraged Grandpa to play whatever piece he was practising at the time. In the living room at Mondaytown, my father preferred to listen with closed eyes, a melody or chord progression inspiring a deep intake of breath or rapturous smile.

Now, once again, we gathered around the Bechstein: a place to play, to sing and to remember. My nephew and niece lifted the keyboard lid and began to strike out robust rhythms: 'Joshua fought the battle of Jericho, Jericho, Jericho, Joshua fought the battle of Jericho and the walls came a-tumbling down.'

Freedom's Soil:
Dvořák at Home and Abroad

At the age of eleven I became a pupil at Chesterton School (now Community College) in Cambridge, a comprehensive school that enjoyed, at that time, a fairly rough reputation. I hadn't been there long when I glanced out of a classroom window to see our geography teacher being chased down the driveway by a dangerous-looking fifth-year pupil. Keeping a low profile was prudent at a school where bullying was prevalent, and discipline a challenge for those teachers who displayed any hint of vulnerability. In an environment where any distinguishing feature – race, accent, sexual orientation, dress sense, unusual surname – was considered fair game for satire, being inconspicuous was a goal I attained most often during football games. Even then my efforts could be spoiled, the sports teacher pointing out my neck 'hickey' to the whole class with a salacious wink: 'Playing the violin – looks like a rough sport to me!'

Nonetheless, there were plenty of teachers who encouraged individual expression. Rex Freeman, an English teacher who could just as well have belonged in a long-established repertory theatre, put on lively plays each year. At the age of thirteen I must have been one of the youngest ever actors to attempt Harold Twine, the sheepish husband in Ben Travers's 1920s farce, *Rookery*

Nook. Non-conformity came at a price, an early attempt at romance scuppered when the girl who was the focus of my bumbling ardour announced that my hairstyle was too embarrassing – perhaps a more general concern conveniently attributed to the middle parting and slicked-back hair that I had assumed for the role.

Chesterton boasted a thriving music programme run by the indefatigable Roger Bond, his name a source of relentless jokes during the era when Roger Moore played the principal part in the James Bond films. Displaying Bondian ingenuity and stamina, Mr Bond accommodated anyone who wanted to play an instrument, forming smaller chamber groups, orchestras, choirs and an impressive number of recorder ensembles. My Chesterton string quartet rehearsed twice a week before school in one of the dank huts close to the school's entrance that had been built as temporary classrooms but somehow became permanent. To be caught up in the lively interplay of voices in an early Haydn quartet is still to be reminded uncomfortably of my teenage self. The transparent textures that expose differences in type of sound, phrase shapes and bow-strokes make Haydn a great choice for a beginner quartet, but on one occasion I reduced our second violinist to tears with an impatient outburst as she struggled to execute a difficult rhythm. Our violist scolded me for intolerant behaviour, an early lesson in the demands of a string quartet, where accountability to three other people was not restricted to one's violin playing.

'Dusinberre! Please refrain from making a fool's pudding of yourself! You should know better than that. *Laudo,* "I praise": Present Indicative Active. *Laudabam,* "I was praising": Imperfect Active. Please pay attention.' Startled from a back-row game of miniature pool, where I had been using a pencil to aim spitballs at the grimy inkwell of my neighbour's wooden desk, I had come up with a confused verb declension for my Latin teacher, Mr Peregrine Maxwell-Stuart. Maxwell-Stuart was an unusual kind of teacher to find at a comprehensive school, where double-barrelled names were treated with suspicion. Although I participated in whispered jokes at the expense of this eccentric teacher whose black three-piece suit matched his haughty focus and attention to detail, secretly I envied his lack of concern with popularity. While I worried whether the Marks & Spencer label that protruded from my generic black pullover would incur the derision of the sophisticated girls in the second row, or whether my last name would again be the subject of embarrassing variation – 'Oi Boysenberry, show us your juicy berries', a less insistent version of the plight suffered in those classes by the unfortunate James Glasscock – Mr Maxwell-Stuart was an unashamedly anachronistic figure, consulting his elegant pocket-watch on a silver chain as the last minutes of each lesson approached. As if he were in an Eton classroom in the early twentieth century rather than a 1980s comprehensive, he seemed determined that the rigorous teaching of Latin should endure. I wondered what it would be like to cultivate his indifference to conformity. One Saturday I was amazed to see him ride past King's College Chapel dressed in a tasselled leather jacket, T-shirt, flared blue jeans and mirror glasses, magnificently unencumbered on a Harley Davidson. No budding Latin scholar, nonetheless I felt mildly ashamed to be considered a fool's pudding by this courageous teacher. I reined in my back-row antics and scraped through the Latin 'O' level exam with a passing grade C.

When I was sixteen years old, I learned the second violin part of Dvořák's 'American' Quartet, with a string quartet comprised of players from the Cambridge Youth Orchestra. Once a month, fellow violinist Bill Hawkes picked up violist John Bass, cellist Richard Beales and myself from our respective homes and drove us one hour south on the M11 to Harlow to be coached by Bill's and my violin teacher: Howard Davis, first violinist of the Alberni Quartet. Independence from parental supervision was joyfully affirmed by Bill's occasional bursts of first-violinist acceleration as he swerved in and out of the fast lane in a red Volkswagen Golf, passing sluggish lorries with a derisive grin.

During one coaching I thought we were conveying adequately the excitement of the final movement until Howard urged John and me to begin the movement with crisper bow-strokes, exaggerating the snapped effect of a dotted rhythm. Played in this way, the second violin and viola provided an irresistible impetus that goaded the first violin to join the party a couple of bars later, with a tune that skipped along to the same rhythm. It was Howard who first told me about Dvořák's love of trains, this repetitive rhythm perhaps an evocation of the journey that he had taken with his family in June 1893 from New York, on his way to spend the summer in the small Czech immigrant community of Spillville, Iowa. The vitality of Dvořák's music, Howard's teaching and the rowdy din that we made driving to his house contributed to an early experience of string quartets as a liberation from the constraints and anxieties of school life.

As part of the centennial programme celebrating Dvořák's summer in Spillville, in July 1993 I travelled there for my first professional engagement with the Takács to perform the 'American' Quartet. Eager to see what remained of the Czech community and the bucolic surroundings that had inspired Dvořák, I was disappointed when our rental car came to stop outside a nondescript motel near the town of Decorah, fifteen miles north-east of Spillville. Later that evening I crossed the busy road outside our motel to dine at the Pizza Hut. For a string quartet with a new first violinist and a sparse concert schedule, saving money on accommodation was more important than savouring a svíčková schnitzel or a twilight walk along the banks of the Turkey river.

The next morning Bill McGlaughlin, the genial yet acute host of the radio show *Saint Paul Sunday*, sat opposite us in front of the ornate icons that surrounded the altar of St Wenceslaus's Catholic Church. At the other end of the aisle, accessible by a narrow spiral staircase, was the same organ that Dvořák had played during his first morning in Spillville, startling worshippers at the usually silent mass with the hymn *Bože, před tvou velebností* ('God before Thy Majesty'). Before we began to play, McGlaughlin surprised me by asking if I would demonstrate the first-violin melody near the beginning of the third movement, which was thought until recently to imitate the scarlet tanager, one of the birds that Dvořák had heard during his early-morning strolls along the river. I played the bird call, fast and high in the violin's register. Without the reassuring framework of the other parts, occasional squeaks and hints of suspect intonation were perhaps faithful to the 5 a.m. call of a bird not yet in best voice but still capable of provoking the dawn chorus. Some time after my shaky rendition, Ted Floyd suggested the red-eyed vireo as a more likely source than the scarlet tanager, citing a field recording captured in Boulder County, Colorado.[1]

My first season in the Takács, following our Spillville visit, was a nerve-racking time for the quartet. As the first non-Hungarian to join the group, I struggled to ignore mutterings among audiences and critics about incompatible national schools of playing. Our New York-based publicist at the time desperately sought a *paprikás*-laden narrative to hide my Englishness and lack of professional experience. The best she could come up with was to describe me as 'a natural linguist', a designation that would have inspired a derisive snort from my former Latin teacher. Eager to counter criticism of an undemonstrative playing style, I looked forward to performing movements of the 'American' Quartet, often offered as encores after more taxing works by Bartók and Brahms. Whether during the slow movement's lament or the unbuttoned high jinks of the finale, the piece that I had first learned in Cambridge enabled me to play with more abandon, a reassuringly familiar ally during a period of adjustment within the group.

On 16 June 1891 Dvořák received a 'lovely doctor's cap and gown' at a ceremony held by the University of Cambridge to grant him an honorary degree. Dvořák was intimidated by the formality of the ritual:

> I listened to my right and to my left and did not know where to turn my ear. And when I discovered that they were talking to me I could have wished myself anywhere else than there and was ashamed that I did not know Latin. But when I look back on it today I must smile and think to myself that to compose *Stabat Mater* is after all, better than to know Latin.[2]

At least for Dvořák. *Stabat Mater*: 'the mother is standing', third-person singular, Imperfect Active Indicative.

The liturgical texts narrating Christ's crucifixion from the point of view of his suffering mother had previously been set to music by composers including Palestrina and Haydn, but Dvořák later admitted that it was hearing requiems by Brahms and Verdi that had inspired him to compose his *Stabat Mater*.[3] Dvořák finished the piece for choir and orchestra in November 1877 under traumatic circumstances, he and his wife Anna Čermáková reeling from the recent loss of their eleven-month-old daughter Růžena from poisoning, and shortly afterwards their first-born son Otakar from smallpox. Their second child Josefa had died two days after her birth in 1875. Even considering the high child mortality rate of the time, it was a cruel beginning to Dvořák and Anna's married life. Between 1878 and 1888 the Dvořáks had another six children, all of whom lived through childhood.

The success of his *Stabat Mater* transformed Dvořák's international profile. After he conducted a performance in March 1883 at the Royal Albert Hall, choral societies in England and America rushed to programme the work. Dvořák's frequent visits to England during the next years included a further performance of the work coupled with the Symphony no. 6 in D minor, Opus 60, at the Worcester Festival in September 1884. The music made a strong impression upon the twenty-seven-year-old Elgar, who played in the first-violin section of the festival orchestra under Dvořák's direction. 'It is simply ravishing, so tuneful & clever & the orchestration is wonderful; no matter how few instruments he uses it never sounds thin.'[4] Writing home to his wife Anna, Dvořák was thrilled by his audience's response: 'Everywhere I appear, whether in the street or at home or even when I go into a shop to buy something, people crowd around me and ask for my autograph. There are pictures of me at all the booksellers' and people buy them only to have some memento.'[5]

Although Dvořák enjoyed the recognition, in accounts of the Cambridge expedition six years later, contrasting aspects of his personality emerged. To the dismay of his host, the composer Charles Villiers Stanford, Dvořák had nearly cancelled the trip from Prague, anxious about the long journey and a raging influenza epidemic. Stanford's bland reassurance that Cambridge was probably healthier than Prague contained little in the way of scientific ballast but was sufficient to persuade the anxious Dvořák to leave home. Although he had been apprehensive about the venture, between the concert and the degree ceremony Dvořák reported to his friend Alois Göbl that the concert had gone splendidly. The Cambridge dons had intimidated Dvořák with their Latin prowess but immediately after his return to Prague Dvořák again wrote to Göbl that everything had turned out splendidly and that he would remember the visit for the rest of his life. The repetition of 'splendid' demonstrated not arrogance but the relief of someone whose anxieties had proven to be ill-founded.

In the same letter Dvořák went on to relay momentous news:

I am to go to America for two years.
The directorship of the Conservatoire and to conduct 10
concerts (of my own compositions) for 8 months and 4
months' vacation, for a yearly salary of 15,000 dollars or
over 30,000 gold francs. Should I take it? Or should I not?[6]

The certainty conveyed by 'I am to go' and the prospect of an annual salary equivalent to more than thirty times what he was making as a teacher at the Prague Conservatory (approximately $400,000 in today's terms) gave way to doubts. The flattering offer of a two-year contract by the visionary president of the National Conservatory, Jeannette Meyer Thurber, was nonetheless daunting. Dvořák worried about how to care for his six children, when exactly he would be paid and whether the obligations of the position would leave him enough time to compose. He asked Göbl to write to him at his summer retreat in the village of Vysoká (Czech for 'high'), located forty-two miles south-west of Prague near the Brdy mountains in a thriving mining region of central Bohemia, where he was about to retreat with his family.

Vysoká was a reassuring place from which the forty-nine-year-old composer could contemplate his options at this critical juncture. Dvořák and Anna had probably first visited Vysoká in 1877 to attend the marriage of Anna's sister Josefína Čermáková to Count Václav Kounic. In 1865, eight years before Dvořák and Anna married, Dvořák had fallen in love with Josefína. It is perhaps fortunate for posterity that she did not return his interest: Dvořák composed eighteen love songs entitled *Cypresses*, settings of poems by Gustav Pfleger Moravský, on the theme of unrequited love.

After Josefína's wedding the Dvořáks visited Vysoká frequently and from 1883 spent entire summers there. In 1884 Kounic sold (or in his descendants' version gave) Dvořák a parcel of land on his country estate that included a sheepfold and a residential house. In May Dvořák wrote to his publisher Simrock: 'I have been here again for some days now in the loveliest woods where I'm spending the most wonderful days in the loveliest weather and am filled with ever new admiration as I listen to the enchanting song of the birds.' Dvořák demolished the sheepfold, salvaging material which was used to build a small caretaker's cottage at the south of the property. He set about adapting the house for himself and his expanding family, adding a crucial element to his study on the upper floor: 'Here in this solitude I shall at last have my own piano – I bought it in Prague for my own money and now I am going with John and a big wagon to fetch it from Příbram.'[7] Dvořák designed his own garden, planting a variety of trees, some chosen especially with the hope of attracting songbirds. In the middle of the garden he built a wooden gazebo that became his favourite place to eat a midday meal, chat with his friends or mark his students' compositions. Some time between 1888 and 1890 Dvořák supervised the addition of an extra wing that included a kitchen, pantry, toilet and porch. In the attic space above the kitchen Dvořák designed a pigeon coop. Breeding pigeons became his most absorbing and therapeutic hobby at Vysoká. To help him maintain the gardens and care for his pigeons, especially during his frequent absences, Dvořák invited the local miner Jan Hodík to live in the new cottage and become his caretaker.[8]

During the autumn of 1891, as Dvořák negotiated the terms of his new position at the National Conservatory, it was important to him that he be allowed to return to Bohemia for his summer holidays. Eventually Dvořák signed a revised contract in December, having decided to travel to New York with Anna and two of his children, entrusting the other four to the care of his mother-in-law. Dvořák's primary duties would be to instruct composition students for two hours a day on Mondays, Wednesdays and Fridays and to conduct two two-hour orchestra rehearsals each week. In his absence Hodík would look after his pigeons, the collection recently augmented by the gift of English pouter and wig pigeons from the British Royal Family.

Dvořák, Anna, Otilka (fourteen) and Antonín (nine) left Bohemia on 15 September 1892, accompanied by Josef Jan Kovařík, a violinist and violist of Czech descent born in Spillville. Kovařík had met Dvořák during his recently completed studies at the Prague Conservatory and agreed to accompany the Dvořák family to New York where he would live with them and work as Dvořák's secretary. Shortly after his arrival in New York, Dvořák wrote to his friend, the lawyer Dr Emil Kozánek:

[W]hen I write to the old country (as they say here) or, what is the same, to every good friend, – being thus engaged with him – it seems to me as if I saw him here before me. And so it is today. I see you, as on a fine autumn morning, walking through the Kroměříž Park and looking sadly at the trees from which the leaves are falling one by one.

Snapping out of his reverie, Dvořák continued:

Our journey was lovely except for one day when everybody on board was sick except me – and so after a short period of quarantine, we arrived safely in the promised land. The view from 'Sandy Hook' (harbour town) – of New York with the magnificent Statue of Liberty (in whose head alone there is room for 60 persons and where banquets etc. are often held) – is most impressive![9]

Before leaving Bohemia, Dvořák had been asked by his new employer Jeannette Thurber to compose a cantata as a contribution to celebrations of the four-hundredth anniversary of Christopher Columbus's so-called discovery of America. Thurber promised to send Dvořák a suitable text but by the time Dvořák received Joseph Rodman Drake's promisingly titled poem, *The American Flag*, he had already acted on a previous suggestion and completed a setting of the Latin liturgical hymn *Te Deum laudamus* ('We praise you God': first-person plural, Present Indicative). In the meantime, Dvořák began work on the new poem, but by the time he arrived in New York he had only been able to write some provisional sketches.

Dvořák could have been in no doubt as to the fervent patriotism of a poem that concluded with the lines:

Where breathes the foe that stands before us
With Freedom's soil beneath our feet,
And Freedom's banner streaming o'er us.[10]

He took several months to finish the piece, the new director of the National Conservatory more interested in the larger project of Thurber's imagining:

The Americans expect great things of me and the main thing is, so they say, to show them to the promised land and kingdom of a new and independent art, in short, to create a new national music. If the small Czech nation can have such musicians, they say, why could not they, too, when the country and people is so immense.[11]

The American Flag would receive its first performance in
Dvořák's absence more than two years later – by which
time the composer's sense of America and his role there
had been transformed by his experiences and circumstances beyond his control.

In *My Antonia*, first published in 1918, Willa Cather
explored the hardship and homesickness facing a Czech
immigrant family as they attempt to settle in Nebraska
in the latter years of the nineteenth century. Early in the
story the patriarch of the family, Mr Shimerda, explains
to his well-meaning neighbours that in Bohemia he and
his family have not always been beggars. Their recent
hardship has been caused by essential expenses associated
with moving to Nebraska: transatlantic passages, train
fares, a homestead, a horse, oxen and farm equipment. As
the winter advances, the new settlers are discouraged by
the severe weather and derelict living quarters that con-
sist of a thatched shed and a small cave, whose makeshift
entrance is an old windmill frame. Mr Shimerda makes
an instant impression on the narrator of the story, Jim
Burden: 'His face was ruggedly formed, but it looked like
ashes – like something from which all the warmth and
light had died out.'[12]

On Christmas Day Mr Shimerda visits the Burdens
at their farm to thank them for their presents. They sit
around the stove, enjoying the warmth and sense of
security.

This feeling seemed completely to take possession of Mr Shimerda. I suppose, in the crowded clutter of their cave, the old man had come to believe that peace and order had vanished from the earth, or existed only in the old world he had left so far behind. He sat still and passive, his head resting against the back of the wooden rocking-chair, his hands relaxed upon the arms. His face had a look of weariness and pleasure, like that of sick people when they feel relief from pain.[13]

A week later Shimerda's daughter Antonia explains to Jim that her father is not well, homesick for Bohemia and his musical friends. At home he used to play the violin constantly for weddings and for dances. But here, even when Antonia pleads with him, he never plays. 'Some days he take his violin out of his box and make with his fingers on the strings, like this, but never he make the music. He don't like this kawn-tree.'[14] To Jim's impatient comment that if he does not like America he would have done better to stay in Bohemia, Antonia retorts that it was her mother who forced them to come, dreaming of American land and wealth. Later in January, one night after dinner, Mr Shimerda shaves, washes himself, puts on a clean shirt and socks, kisses his children goodnight and walks to the barn. After hanging his coat on a peg, placing his boots under the bed and folding his silk neckcloth, he shoots himself in the head with a rifle.

Shimerda's family and neighbours discuss where to bury a man whose suicide will probably exclude him from the Catholic cemetery. The officers of a nearby Norwegian church hold a meeting and refuse to accommodate him. Mrs Shimerda and her son Ambrosch wish to bury him at a corner of their land. Several days later Jim Burden's grandfather prays over Mr Shimerda's freshly dug grave, asking forgiveness of anyone who has 'been remiss toward the stranger come to a far country'.[15] Shimerda's widow requests a hymn and everyone in the assembled party begins to sing 'Jesus, Lover of my Soul'. Too late, Mr Shimerda gets the music he had been yearning for. His inability to play the violin is Cather's most poignant symbol of a broken heart.

Dvořák's first days in New York had little in common with Mr Shimerda's desolate experience. The celebrated composer and his family were met at the port of Hoboken by an enthusiastic delegation of Czech citizens and people associated with the National Conservatory before being installed in luxurious rooms at the Hotel Clarendon near Union Square, on the corner of Fourth Avenue and East 18th Street. The presence of a new Steinway grand piano was not enough to distract Dvořák from the unaccustomed noise of the city. Kovařík was swiftly dispatched to find cheaper long-term accommodation. The house on East 17th Street where Dvořák would live for the remainder of his New York sojourn was within

easy walking distance of the Conservatory, overlooking
Stuyvesant Square in a vibrant neighbourhood whose
population included Russian Jewish, German and Irish
immigrants.

Dvořák was first presented on 9 October at a Czech
concert in his honour attended by around three thousand
people who clapped and cheered with abandon. 'There
were speeches in Czech and English and I, poor crea-
ture, had to make a speech of thanks from the platform,
holding a silver wreath in my hands. You can guess how
I felt.' Despite the festive occasion, his anxiety was compounded by the American newspapers' description of
him as the 'saviour of music and I don't know what all
else besides!'[16]

On 21 October the National Conservatory presented
another concert honouring Dvořák at Carnegie Hall
(which had officially opened on 5 May 1891), a continua-
tion also of ongoing Columbus anniversary celebrations.
Dvořák conducted the New York Philharmonic in three of
his overtures, *In Nature's Realm*, *Carnival* and *Othello*, and
the *Te Deum*, composed for the occasion. This time the
speechifying was assigned to Colonel Thomas Wentworth
Higginson, an author, abolitionist and ordained Unitarian
minister perhaps best known for his friendship with
Emily Dickinson, whom he served as editor and adviser.
Had Dvořák himself been giving the oration, it is unlikely
that he would have aired Higginson's erroneous view
that music had not existed in America before Columbus's

arrival. Dvořák's awareness of Native American culture probably dated back to an article, 'Songs of the American Indian', written by his friend V. J. Novotný, and his discovery of Longfellow's poem *Hiawatha* in a Czech translation, several years before his journey to America. As soon as he arrived in New York, Jeannette Thurber conveyed her enthusiastic wish that her protégé compose an opera based on *Hiawatha*.

The idea that music only existed in America after Columbus's arrival was consistent with prevalent attitudes towards Native Americans, who had suffered the seizure of their lands by white settlers expanding westwards, an advance so comprehensive that settler and future president Theodore Roosevelt complained in 1892: 'The frontier proper has come to an end.'[17] Where next for those like Roosevelt who felt expansionism to be an essential feature of national identity? Even Willa Cather's poignant account of Mr Shimerda's plight was a one-sided portrayal of displacement. Between 1825 and 1892 Native American tribes including the Arapaho, Cheyenne, Missouri, Omaha, Oto and Pawnee all ceded land in Nebraska to the US government in eighteen separate treaties. The stories of Native Americans forced to leave their homes were given much less attention than the challenges that European successors experienced adapting to their new environment.

In November 1892 Dvořák reported that he was still enjoying New York very much but conceded that there were things he would prefer not to see, referring to the squalid and desperate living conditions he observed on his daily walks. Ending his summary on an upbeat note, he was unaware of a crisis in the New Year that would have longer-term repercussions for both the National Conservatory and those already living on the brink: 'In general, however, it is altogether different here, and, if America goes on like this, she will surpass all the others.'[18]

He had reason to be optimistic. Thurber's assignment of *The American Flag* belied her nuanced and often visionary ideas about music education. After opening the National Conservatory in 1885, she frequently bolstered its budget from her own pocket to keep tuition fees low. She encouraged gifted students who could not afford to pay tuition to sign an agreement stating that after graduation they would, for a limited time, contribute a quarter of their annual professional earnings above $1,000 to the Conservatory. Thanks to Thurber's persistent recruitment philosophy, the Conservatory gained a reputation before Dvořák's arrival for having an unusually high intake of both female and black students – a trend that would later be reflected in the composition of its faculty.

Dvořák's interest in the music of black composers flourished in this environment. On 21 May 1893 an unsigned article in the *New York Herald* presented his ideas about the future of American music: 'In the Negro melodies of America I discover all that is needed for a great and noble school of music. They are pathetic, tender, passionate, melancholy, solemn, religious, bold, merry, gay or what you will . . .'[19] Michael Beckerman has argued convincingly that the article was one of several most likely written about Dvořák by the journalist James Creelman.[20] Dvořák offered no complaint at being represented in this way, indeed endorsing the article in a letter written to the editors of the newspaper the following week, his exact words however again most probably sculpted by Creelman.

At the National Conservatory Dvořák was fortunate to meet Harry T. Burleigh, a baritone and composer who had grown up in Erie, Pennsylvania. Burleigh was the grandson of Hamilton Waters, a slave in Somerset County, Maryland, who after purchasing his freedom in 1832 settled in Erie, an important place on the Underground Railroad in which Waters was involved. As a young boy Harry first heard stories and songs of plantation life when he accompanied his grandfather on his rounds as a lamplighter. Burleigh developed his talents as a singer both in church and at home and at the age of twenty-five left Erie for New York to apply to the National Conservatory. He became a student a few months before Dvořák assumed the position of director.

Burleigh recalled many hours spent at Dvořák's house where, in the company of thrushes that flew from the open doors of their cages throughout the house, he introduced Dvořák to spirituals including 'Nobody Knows the Trouble I've Seen', 'Go Down Moses' and 'Swing Low,

Sweet Chariot'. While Dvořák's guidance of Burleigh, Will Marion Cook, Laura Sedgwick Collins, Paul Bolin, Maurice Arnold and others encouraged the emergence of a generation of black composers, their music had a profound effect on his own artistic development, particularly on the piece that would become his most successful work. The Symphony no. 9, 'From the New World', composed between January and May 1893, was shaped by his close association with Burleigh. In preparation for the first performance of the new symphony, Burleigh copied out many of the orchestral parts. More significantly, he provided a source of inspiration: Dvořák drew on features of 'Swing Low, Sweet Chariot' for the final theme of his first movement.

A National Conservatory concert to benefit the *New York Herald*'s Free Clothing Drive on 23 January 1894 highlighted aspects of Thurber's vision, featuring African American singers Burleigh and Sissieretta Jones accompanied by the Conservatory's orchestra and chorus. Another student, Maurice Arnold, conducted the premiere of his composition *Plantation Dances*. The concert offered a precedent for more inclusive programming, but although Dvořák played his part in attempting to realise Thurber's goals, over the next decades racist attitudes would impede their wider implementation. While African American students struggled to make progress within the stifling hierarchy of the classical music profession, the 'New World' Symphony became Dvořák's most famous and successful work. The 'promised land' bestowed its good fortune selectively.

Dvořák's work at the National Conservatory and his increased recognition as a composer did not prevent sudden intrusions of homesickness. Vysoká was on his mind when he wrote to his caretaker, Jan Hodík, in March 1893:

I would be delighted if you would describe to me everything you have been doing there and how it is all going. Have you moved any shrubs and, if so, where have you put them? What about those young fruit trees, wouldn't it be better to prune any superfluous branches so that the trees are better able to grow?[21]

Missing his pigeons, Dvořák visited the large aviary at the Zoological Gardens in Central Park. According to Kovařík, they made the expedition to Central Park at least once a week.

If caring for pigeons with their powerful homing instincts satisfied one aspect of Dvořák's temperament, his obsession with trains spoke to a more restless side. Ever since the age of nine when he had observed the construction of a new railway track linking Prague and Dresden, Dvořák had been fascinated by trains that suggested a world of possibility beyond the confines of village life in Nelahozeves, twenty-two miles north-west of Prague. Throughout his adult life, on early-morning walks Dvořák liked to head for the bridge near Prague's main railway station, from where he could observe the trains leaving the city. The avid train-spotter took note of engine numbers and chatted in the station with drivers about the latest technological innovations. While planning his international trips, Dvořák enjoyed studying the timetables to craft the best available schedule. When Dvořák sent his student (and future son-in-law) Josef Suk to record the engine number of an express train to Vienna, the novice disappointed his teacher by instead returning with the number of the tender at the rear of the train. Fortunately for Dvořák's New York students, train-spotting opportunities in New York were limited. Despite Kovařík's entreaties to a porter at the main station, only passengers were allowed onto the platform. After travelling by tram one hour north of their house to the 155th Street station, Dvořák and Kovařík could wait on a bank above the tracks to catch a glimpse of the Chicago or Boston express. Dvořák turned his attention to the steamers that transported his letters back to friends and family in Bohemia, taking advantage of opportunities for members of the public to board and inspect the ships in the harbour, where he would strike up conversations with their captains and mates. If he became so absorbed in his work at the Conservatory as to miss the departure of a ship from the harbour, Kovařík recalled that they took the overhead tram to Battery Park, the most southerly point of Manhattan, following the ship's progress from there until it was out of sight.[22]

Despite his yearning for Bohemia, over the course of spring 1893 Dvořák delayed his plan to return there for the summer, in part in order to finish work on his Symphony no. 9. In the meantime Kovařík invited Dvořák and his family back to spend the summer with his own family in his home town of Spillville. Dvořák arranged for his sister-in-law Terezie Koutecká to bring his remaining four children from Prague to New York, enthusiastic about 'our summer Vysoká . . . where the teacher and the parish priest and everything is Czech and so I shall be among my own folks'.[23] On 3 June, three days after the family reunited in New York, the party set out for Spillville on the express train to Chicago.

Dvořák enjoyed the long journey, curious about the countryside as the train passed through Philadelphia, Harrisburg and the Allegheny mountains, the mood only spoiled when he discovered that the state law of Pennsylvania forbade the sale of alcohol on trains: 'So this is America, the land of freedom! Free country! And one cannot even get a glass of beer here! You should see how one travels in Russia. The train there moves for half an hour, then stops for an hour, and you can comfortably eat and drink.'[24] If Dvořák's outburst was an unconvincing advertisement for Russian trains, he had seen enough during his first year in New York to realise that American life was not as straightforward as portrayed in Drake's *The American Flag*. Following a period of rapid expansion in the railroad business financed by unsustainable debt, a declaration of bankruptcy by the Philadelphia and Reading Railroad on 20 February 1893 was one of several events that preceded the failure of banks and thousands of businesses. On 3 May the stock market crashed. A catastrophic drop in wheat prices and a devastating increase in the number of people unemployed signalled the onset of a depression that would last for several years. The Czech party sped westwards over 'freedom's soil' with 'freedom's banner streaming overhead', in the words of *The American Flag*, as yet unaware of the danger that these events would pose to Dvořák's American project.

On his first morning in Spillville, Dvořák arose early and went for a walk by the Turkey river: 'Imagine, I was walking there in the wood along the stream and after eight months I heard again the singing of the birds! And here the birds are different from ours, they have much brighter colours and they sing differently, too.'[25] His son Otakar later recalled that for a boy hoping to fish, the surroundings provided rather too much musical inspiration: one trip down to the river was abruptly curtailed when he was told to hurry home so that his father could write down all his ideas. Within a few days Dvořák had already sketched out the 'American' Quartet. He completed the piece within three weeks, his progress aided by an in-house string quartet. Kovařík reported that the whole family applied itself to the exciting assignment of playing this music immediately after Dvořák had composed it: Dvořák took the first violin part, Kovařík's father the second, his sister the viola and Kovařík the cello part.[26]

In the midst of the Bohemian immigrant community Dvořák was happier than in New York, but by the end of the summer his perspective had changed. He wrote to Emil Kozánek, the same correspondent to whom he had admiringly described the Statue of Liberty after first arriving in New York:

It is very strange here. Few people and a great deal of empty space. A farmer's nearest neighbour is often four miles off, especially in the *prairies* (I call them the Sahara) there are only endless acres of field and meadow and that is all you see. You don't meet a soul (here they only ride on horseback) and you are glad to see in the woods and meadows the huge herds of cattle which, summer and winter, are at pasture in the broad fields. Men go to the woods and meadows where the cows graze to milk them. And so it is very 'wild' here and sometimes very sad – sad to despair.[27]

Twenty-five years before Cather published *My Antonia*, Dvořák was thinking of the hardships and struggles of his countrymen during their first years in Spillville, probably unaware that in the first half of the nineteenth century the Turkey river that provided musical inspiration had served as a departure point for members of the Sioux, Sauk, Winnebago and Fox tribes, forced to leave

Iowa as a result of federal government violence and ensuing treaties aimed at clearing swathes of land for white settlers. But while living in Spillville, Dvořák sensed an underlying alienation and loneliness, 'sad to despair', an emotion that he conveyed powerfully in the slow movement of his new quartet.

Playing the 'American' Quartet in the Queen's Hall at the 2018 Edinburgh Festival, my view of the piece was affected by a period of change within the Takács. After forty-three years of characterful and committed playing, founding second violinist Károly Schranz had recently retired from the group.* In just a couple of months, Harumi Rhodes, our friend and colleague at the University of Colorado, had assumed her new role with panache, humour and flexibility. Nonetheless, violist Geri Walther had recently announced that after fifteen seasons of playing over eighty quartet concerts a year, she would leave the group in May 2020, shortly before her seventieth birthday. Siegmund Nissel, second violinist of the Amadeus Quartet, once compared a string quartet to a fine wine: if the cellist was the bottle and the first violin the label, the inner voices were the beverage. While I sometimes thought of myself as more like the cork than the label – culpable when the wine smelled off – there

---

* Károly's crucial role within the quartet is described in more detail in my previous book, *Beethoven for a Later Age: The Journey of a String Quartet*.

was no doubting the importance of Geri and Károly's vibrant voices in the midst of the group: to refashion the quartet would be a serious undertaking.

Questions concerning the quartet's musical identity had first been highlighted after my arrival and again after Englishman Roger Tapping became our violist in 1995. The 'Anglo-Magyar foursome' proved a convenient label for the next decade until Geri joined the group in 2005 – just so long as we were deemed to sound more Hungarian than English. To relentless questions about how two Englishmen and two Hungarians managed to work together, Roger was tempted to answer that although we had at first employed a translator for rehearsals, now unfortunately we could no longer afford one. We invented an emblematic if dubious-sounding meal of *gulyás* and chips. Not everyone was convinced by the mish-mash of nationalities, the distinguished music critic Tully Potter complaining of 'a patchwork of playing styles'.[28]

Of the founding Hungarian members of the quartet that had formed in Budapest in 1975, only András now remained. Under such circumstances, to potter along pining for our Hungarian roots seemed like a questionable strategy. One of the things I loved about András's playing was a lack of ego that reminded me of my grandpa's approach to music: András's noble, understated approach to cello melodies brought the music rather than the performer to the fore. During the ups and downs that inevitably occur over the course of a long career, my sometimes volatile first reactions to setbacks were balanced by András's steadiness and, dare I say it, stiff upper lip – an improbable manifestation of his inner Brit. As we began to consider who might be suitable to join a Hungarian cellist, English/American first violinist and Japanese/Jewish-American second violinist, our best hope was that a patchwork of styles could be fashioned into a varied yet unified quilt, national stereotypes of little value within the group.

Conflicting emotions surface during the extended transition that usually occurs when a quartet is looking for a new player. Both for the person leaving and for those who remain, sorrow at the imminent cessation of one series of quartet relationships keeps uneasy company with excitement and anxiety about the future. Geri had shown courage in deciding to leave the group when she was still playing at her very best but the prospect of her departure so soon after Harumi had joined the group made it difficult for the four of us to explore a new voice together – instead we were in a holding pattern, three of us anxious about the future direction of the group.

During our Edinburgh concert I was grateful to hide behind Dvořák's vibrant music. At the beginning of the 'American' Quartet my offbeat *pianissimo* entrance, followed by Harumi's imitation a sixth lower, created the sense of a long upbeat, each of us oscillating between two notes in a shimmer of semiquavers that evoked a sunrise. András's upbeat quaver preceded the first articulated downbeat of the piece, a pedal-note F that set the scene for Geri's melody, in which syncopation and snapping dotted rhythms combined with sweeping lyricism; hopeful music that crackled with energy and purpose. Encouraged by the warm acoustics of the Queen's Hall, I gave my first-violin melodies in the slow movement a generous dollop of vibrato, enjoying throughout how the accompanying figures reacted to the ebb and flow, and the shape of the melodies. I played the bird imitation in the third movement with more confidence than in Spillville twenty-five years ago, if still not entirely in tune. Towards the end of the exhilarating finale, Geri played with maximum energy to project above exuberant chords and driving triplets. We ended with an ecstatic unison declamation of the same dotted rhythm that dominated the movement, followed by three emphatic chords. The gratifying roar of audience approval that greeted this ending had as much to do with Dvořák's ingenuity as the skill of the performers.

After the concert a less obvious passage continued to play in my head. Two-thirds of the way through the first movement the opening melody returned with subtle differences. Although the violins' semiquavers and the contours of Geri's tune were recognisable, Harumi and I were now marked *ppp* – almost inaudible. Instead of underpinning the group with a pedal note, András stopped playing, contributing merely an offbeat pizzicato in the second bar of Geri's melody that now began more quietly. The hushed dynamics and the absence of a bass note contributed to the melody's more speculative mood; after a stormy and dramatic section in the minor key it returned like a character in a play re-entering the stage tentatively, wondering what has changed. Whereas after its first appearance in the piece the melody culminated in a joyful *forte*, now it headed in a different direction altogether, András offering a variation on an earlier lyrical theme, this time in the remote key of D flat major. The overall effect was to downplay the significance of the return and in so doing question the mood of the theme: expectancy and purpose were replaced by music more cautious and exploratory.

Following our Edinburgh Festival concert, my attitude to the slow movement of the piece was swayed by the ideas of the Takács's newest member. Rather than representing an impassioned outpouring in the moment, Harumi understood the sadness as something that had happened already: there should be nothing hot, juicy or urgent about this 'weathered' sorrow. Rather than 'listen to me', she imagined the melody being played with a different attitude: 'whether you listen or not this still remains the story'. Harumi's idea had corresponding implications for the accompaniment: the repeated rhythms could be more objective, a landscape detached from the dynamic shaping of the melody. If the collective sound was too rich, the melody had no space to be lonely.

I recalled the letter Dvořák had written from Spillville to Emil Kozánek: 'And so it is very "wild" here and sometimes very sad – sad to despair.' In Dvořák's observation of how insignificant humans were in this vast landscape, I understood Harumi's idea of an accompaniment as a backbone, not easily swayed by the emotional fluctuations of the melody. Now I noticed an earlier part of Dvořák's letter that I had skimmed over before. He wrote that when passing by the grave of Joseph Spielmann, the German founder of Spillville who had died four years before Dvořák's visit, 'strange thoughts always fill my mind at the sight of it as of the graves of many other Czech countrymen who sleep their last sleep there'.[29] Had Cather allowed Mr Shimerda to land in the less bleak environment of Spillville, perhaps he would have raised his violin to play a tune that evoked wistful memories of his countrymen. If the light had gone out in Mr Shimerda's eyes, in my version of Dvořák's melody perhaps it burned too brightly.

While homesickness was one source of inspiration for this slow movement, Harry T. Burleigh provided another. When he sang African American spirituals learned from his grandfather to Dvořák, Burleigh conveyed the collective grief caused by so many generations of cruelty, oppression and the relentless erosion of human dignity. 'Nobody knows the trouble I've been through, Lord. Nobody knows my sorrow.' There was nothing sentimental about a sorrow known only to the Lord, ongoing and reconciled only by a different kind of homecoming:

If you get there before I do
Oh, yes, Lord
Tell all-a my friends I'm coming to Heaven!
Oh, yes, Lord[30]

Harumi's questions about our interpretation of the slow movement extended to the piece as a whole, music so familiar to performers and audiences alike that there was a tendency to caricature its emotions, to assume that in a given moment the music communicated only one prevailing mood: a first movement upbeat and folksy, a cathartic slow movement dripping with sadness and a last movement played with maximum tempo and energy to provoke foot-stomping applause.

As I began to read the ballads from Karel Jaromír Erben's anthology, *A Bouquet*, which provided inspiration throughout Dvořák's life, his visit to the graveyard in Spillville took on more significance. Dvořák had first set Erben's 'Wedding Shirts' as *The Spectre's Bride*. In the aria 'Where art thou, Father dear?', featured in Dvořák's Cambridge concert of June 1891, a desperate young woman grieving the loss of both parents, her sister and brother, prays to the Virgin Mary for the safe return of her lover.

I, sad and forlorn, had a lover,
His life than my own was dearer,
Gone is he now across the sea,
Nor has he yet returned to me.[31]

When the young woman expresses the thought that without her lover she would prefer not to live, her suicide wish is a sin against the Catholic faith of Dvořák's upbringing and serves as the catalyst for the return of a corpse masquerading as the girl's actual lover. This apparition convinces her to leave her home and embark on a breathless and terrifying nocturnal journey that takes up much of the cantata.

Listening to the music alone, I would have guessed that the climactic phrase of a duet where the girl and her assumed lover sing in octaves was an ecstatic consummation. In fact, although they sing the same melody, their differing words revealed an opposition, the corpse urging his victim along while the girl protested that she was weak and could not continue. Perhaps this dramatic use of a tune emphasised the persuasive powers of the corpse.[32] It might be harsh to compare the ambitious Mrs Shimerda, urging her husband to leave Bohemia for the promised land, to a devious corpse, but the dichotomy was the same: one person forcing a journey on a fearful and reluctant companion. In Dvořák's imagination, journeys were fraught with the dangers more severe than the absence of alcohol on a train in Pennsylvania.

At the denouement of the cantata the corpse exclaims to the young woman that they are finally home at his castle and orchard. Her suspicions have been aroused: instead of the home she has been dreaming of, she sees only a church and its graveyard. The corpse instructs her to leap over the graveyard wall but the young woman tricks him, asking him to jump first and then escaping into the shelter of a small morgue. Her rescue is completed when she prays to the Virgin Mary to forgive her sin and save her from this evil power. The chorus and baritone narrator conclude that things would have turned out much worse if she had not asked for help from God.

To read Erben's ballads was to experience a complexity and darkness not so immediately apparent in the 'American' Quartet. From Spillville Dvořák wrote that he was planning to 'delve' into 'Zahor's Bed', a tale at least as grim as *The Spectre's Bride*. He mentioned the project again in November after his return to New York. Although he did not after all set 'Zahor's Bed' to music, he returned to Erben's stories two years later in Bohemia, once again to encounter tormented characters who lived through the consequences of their poor decisions and, if they were fortunate, were granted forgiveness.

Like a person I thought I knew well, I had pigeonholed Dvořák. To my students I often suggested that they infuse Dvořák's music with more sense of informality, evoking village dances and early-morning walks by the river. My point of view had something in common with that of the music critic Henry Krehbiel, who after hearing the first New York performance in January 1894 of the 'American' Quartet and String Quintet in E flat, also written in Spillville, found Dvořák's music to be 'full of ingenuity, replete with gracious fancy, clear as crystal and inspiriting in its unalloyed happiness'.[33] But to emphasise unalloyed happiness was perhaps to limit the possibilities in these generally cheerful Spillville works. My view of Dvořák had been skewed by early, joyful associations with the piece. By stereotyping Dvořák as a breath of fresh air, a more entertaining musical companion guaranteed to provide relief from the weightier fare of Bartók and Beethoven, I was not allowing him the capacity for ambiguity. In the latter part of his American sojourn, dichotomies in Dvořák's life and music were often entwined with departures and homecomings.

Anton Seidl, the conductor of the first performance of Dvořák's Symphony no. 9 on 16 December 1893 in Carnegie Hall, did not like the title 'New World' Symphony: he felt the music conveyed a yearning for home.[34] Homesickness was one of the work's predominant features for a Hungarian immigrant who had moved to New York in 1891 to become conductor of the New York Philharmonic. Dvořák had finished the work in New York before he travelled west to Spillville. Nonetheless Seidl placed the slow movement's loneliness among the settlers and prairies of the Midwest, a context also suggested by Willa Cather when she reviewed a performance of the work in 1897 given by the Pittsburgh Symphony Orchestra. As Mr Shimerda had found out, homesickness could be overwhelming when the hopes and dreams inspired by a new world were not realised.

During the premiere of the piece in Carnegie Hall, the applause after the slow movement was so insistent that Dvořák, sitting at the back of a box on the second tier, eventually stood up to acknowledge the ovation, inspiring a writer for the *New York Herald* to offer a character portrayal of sorts:

He is dark. Dark hair, scanty upon the top. A dark, short beard, fast becoming gray. Dark eyes, wide open with a cheerful steady look in them – a look which from time to time changes into a faraway regard that has somewhat of pathos in it. The face is honest, kindly and with a general expression of perfectly guileless nature.[35]

The reviewer, overly reliant on 'dark' to describe his subject, was not alone in observing pathos. After Dvořák returned to New York from Spillville, his son Otakar noticed that his father's fragile nerves and tendencies towards depression had become more troublesome. Now Otakar had a new assignment – to accompany his father to the Conservatory. At times his father feared the tram's electric wire, wagons or other street vehicles.[36] One student remarked on Dvořák's frantic terror during thunderstorms. His performance anxiety was extreme in the build-up to a concert, walks around Stuyvesant Square doing little to alleviate restlessness. The situation was worse when Dvořák was thinking about a new work but not yet composing it. At these times, according to his assistant Kovařík, he was often 'difficult to understand, bad tempered or distraught'.[37]

Dvořák yearned for Bohemia and Vysoká. He wrote to his caretaker Jan Hodík, asking if the pigeons were getting enough food, suggesting that he let the young doves fly out of the coop as long as they were well behaved. In January Dvořák asked Hodík to report back on a damaged wall, complaining that time was passing slowly in New York. Hodík's daughter had recently died and Hodík had been very ill himself. Perhaps rating the therapeutic powers of pigeons too highly, Dvořák suggested that if nothing else, Hodík could be cheered up by talking to them. Stuck in New York, Dvořák again urged Hodík to let the healthy young doves fly out from their coop. Dvořák's pain at being so far away from home was exacerbated by the death of his father on 28 March 1894. Distraught at having missed the funeral, Dvořák asked his sister to keep his father's zither and other mementos until his return to Bohemia in May.

Jeannette Thurber had ample opportunity to observe her employee's homesickness, but might not have concurred with the *New York Herald* writer's assumption about his guileless nature. As a result of the national financial crisis, she was having trouble paying Dvořák's salary. A transfer of $7,500, already three months late, finally reached his Prague bank in December 1893, but was not honoured. The problematic situation rumbled on until in April 1894 Dvořák threatened to expose the breach of contract. He was conscious enough of his fame to think that such a delay would create a scandal, even during a national financial crisis when people might arguably have more urgent concerns than the plight of a famous composer. Thurber took her chances, waiting for two weeks before sending him $2,000 and offering a two-year extension of his contract through spring 1896, furthermore judging as 'rather unkind' his initial refusal to sign until she had paid all monies owed to him. Dvořák softened his position, accepting a written promise that the $7,500 would be paid before 6 October. He signed a new contract, happily contemplating a summer in Vysoká and grateful for Thurber's dispensation that he need not be back in New York until November.

On 30 May 1894 Dvořák arrived in Prague with his wife and children. Crowds gathered at the station to get a glimpse of the composer. Two days later Dvořák continued his journey to Vysoká, again to be greeted by local friends who accompanied him to the local inn, eager to hear tales of his adventures abroad. To celebrate his return Dvořák ordered and paid for a new organ for the church in the neighbouring village of Třebsko. On 8 September, when a full congregation celebrated Dvořák's birthday, the priest Matej Novák recalled that his usually steadfast worshippers had paid more attention to the organ donor than to the altar. Everyone participated in singing the hymn 'A Thousand

Times We Greet You'. Novák noticed that Dvořák introduced many new notes and chords during the service, surmising that this was to test the capabilities of the new organ. Absent from the celebrations was his father, whom Dvořák described shortly after his death as one of his most treasured sources of happiness.[38] Whatever his motivation for adapting melodies and chord progressions during the church service, changes to at least one of his later compositions would reflect an awareness of loss, intensified by homecomings.

A restful summer did little to improve Dvořák's mental state following his return to New York in October 1894. This time he was accompanied only by Anna and his youngest son Otakar, his anxiety increased by the family being split up. Still afraid to walk alone in the city, Dvořák kept copious notes in his notebook of news from home, listing also the names of the ships that took his own letters back to Prague. Further affecting his mood in November was news of his sister-in-law Josefína's ill health. As he composed the slow movement of a new cello concerto, Dvořák returned to 'Leave Me Alone', one of his melodies from Opus 82, a song that according to his son-in-law (the inept train-spotter Josef Suk) was one of Josefína's favourites. This song shared some characteristics with an earlier song from *Cypresses*, the cycle that Dvořák had composed for Josefína in 1865. For the rhapsodic and at times turbulent middle section, Dvořák passed over the luminous opening phrase of 'Leave Me

Alone', choosing instead the stormier melodic line that
moves to a minor key in the second stanza:

Leave me alone! Do not dispel the peace
Within my breast with your loud words![39]

Scurrying violins play a rhythm that seems to agitate the
cello melody. The flute and oboe take over the tune in dialogue with the cello. Compared with the earlier song, the
melody is given more room to expand, moving through
different keys that signal unstable shifts of mood. When
the clarinet plays the theme the cello provides the underlying agitation, arpeggiated figures that necessitate the
physical effort of string crossings, the cellist straining
over the instrument to reach notes uncomfortably high
in the register. Eventually the emotion exhausts itself
with a series of descending sighs.

Dvořák thought he had finished the piece in New
York. On 16 April 1895 he once more left New York
with Anna and Otakar to spend the summer in Bohemia,
perhaps not heartbroken to miss by a couple of weeks
the premiere of *The American Flag*. After Josefína's death
in May, Dvořák decided to work again on the end of the
Cello Concerto, adding sixty bars to incorporate the
previously ignored first phrase of the song 'Leave Me
Alone'. Dvořák now introduced the phrase as a high violin solo, the solo cello at first suspended on one note,
listening to the violin, then soaring high in its register

as it echoed the melodic line: 'Leave me alone in my fond dream to go'.

Outraged that cellist Hanuš Wihan planned to add his own cadenza to the end of the piece, Dvořák explained his thinking about this revised conclusion to his publisher:

> The finale closes gradually diminuendo, like a sigh – with reminiscences of the I. and II. Movements – the solo dies down to pp, (– then swells again –) and the last bars are taken up by the orchestra and the whole concludes in a stormy mood. – That was my idea and I cannot depart from it.[40]

The possibility that Dvořák continued to harbour romantic feelings for Josefína throughout her life is intriguing but difficult to substantiate. More tangible were the ways in which Dvořák's changed life circumstances were reflected in his musical language, in the adaptation of older melodies, and the reimagining of musical forms.

Apart from revising the ending of the Cello Concerto, Dvořák enjoyed a lazy summer. Although Thurber had expected him to return to New York again the following autumn, she received instead a resignation letter written on 17 August, signed by both Dvořák and his wife Anna. Dvořák explained to Thurber that Anna's mother was now too old to take care of their children, Anna did not wish to be separated from them again and the children's education was a priority. Just three weeks before his fifty-fourth birthday, Dvořák did not mention his own emotional fragility, exacerbated by being away from home, nor the fact that Thurber still could not afford to pay his full salary – an additional factor in bringing Dvořák's American adventure to an end.

As he settled into his life in Vysoká, Dvořák had time to study the domestic environment of his treasured pigeons. To his son Otakar, Dvořák observed that a pigeon cooed differently depending on the circumstances, whether being angry with a neighbour, courting or conversing with a mate.[41] In order to tackle the problem of pigeons abandoning their nests, Dvořák instructed Hodík to have boards prepared by the local joiner so as to create partitions between pairs of pigeons. Dvořák ascended a ladder

to observe the effect of this new design, delighted that they took to the new arrangement and shortly began to nest.

The English and German titles of Dvořák's *The Wild Dove/ Die Waldtaube* (also sometimes known in English as *The Wood Dove*), one of four symphonic poems composed in 1896, acknowledge an undomesticated bird far removed from Dvořák's pigeons nesting within their partitioned coop. These symphonic poems follow the stories of K. J. Erben's ballads in the form of orchestral pieces without words or singers. At the beginning of *Holoubek* – to give the work its Czech title – a young widow grieves her husband as she accompanies his coffin to the graveside. Precipitously sorrow gives way to joy: she has in fact poisoned her husband and within a month marries a younger man. Three years later, above her murdered husband's grave a white dove sits on a young oak tree. The woman pleads with the dove to stop its lament, to leave her alone, but its insistent song is a piercing reminder of her sin that drives her mad – to escape its voice she drowns herself in a river.

The Wild Dove begins with the dotted rhythm of a funeral march – no longer a train speeding westwards to Iowa – accompanying a mournful, chromatic melody. The melody is put to work in extraordinary ways. The entrance of the young man, an exuberant wedding feast, a wedding waltz, the mourning song of the dove played at first by the bass clarinet and a climax that signifies the murderess's insanity are all encapsulated by variations of this one theme. In both Erben's ballad and Dvořák's orchestral setting, the dove's song derails the young woman. Near the end of his piece Dvořák departs from Erben's tale by introducing a redemptive variation of the melody played by the solo violin. What would Erben have made of this positive twist to his ending? The poet does not allow any such resolution: a curse will weigh more heavily over the protagonist than the stone that covers her grave. In Dvořák's version the last chords climb up to a peaceful C major resolution.

After his return to Bohemia Dvořák seemed to be attempting to lay voices to rest, searching for a resolution comprised of many elements. In this later work, Dvořák fashioned a satisfying musical unity from Erben's grim story. Using his words as a starting point, Dvořák harnessed the ability of music to collect grief, celebration, guilt, madness and reconciliation, all under one roof.

Turning the Page

'Dvořák Doesn't Live Here Anymore', declared a *New York Times* headline on 7 March 1991. Unbeknown to me a battle was waged during my first year studying in New York, over the future of the house on East 17th Street where Dvořák had lived between 1892 and 1895. In 1989, the year that the number of reported AIDS cases in America reached 100,000, the Beth Israel Medical Center had bought the house, intending to build a twenty-eight-bed AIDS hospice in its place. Following a campaign by local activists, the Landmarks Commission decided to thwart the plans by designating the house a historic landmark. The *New York Times* was unimpressed:

> The original stoop is gone. What was once the front door is now a kitchen window. A spiral staircase cuts the parlor floor in half and rooms have been partitioned and repartitioned. The commission made the building a landmark not for its physical attributes but as a kind of historical memory bank. That raises the prospect of a city dotted with shrines because a celebrity passed through. New York City, which has always attracted the notable, cannot turn every site of sentimental interest

into a landmark, protected from demolition and even most exterior changes.[1]

Three months later, a performance by bass-baritone William Wakefield of William Arms Fisher's song 'Goin' Home' – an arrangement of the main melody from the *Largo* of the 'New World' Symphony – was not enough to dissuade the New York City Council from overruling the Landmark Commission's designation. Following the demolition of the house the much-needed hospice was built for AIDS patients. Preservationists and Dvořák enthusiasts redirected their energies, looking for ways to save remnants of the house and move them to a new location. Architect Jan Hird Pokorny salvaged several sections from two mantelpieces and combined them to make a single prominent feature in a new Dvořák room in the same building as the Bohemian Concert Hall on East 73rd Street, under the auspices of the Dvořák American Heritage Association. Cultural historian Majda Kallab Whitaker set out to recreate the atmosphere and dimensions of a Victorian parlour by adding a period desk and a lighting fixture from the 1890s. A large signed portrait of Dvořák was placed on the wall.

One of the last pieces that Dvořák had begun in the house on East 17th Street was his String Quartet in A flat major, Opus 105. In March 1895, occupied with his teaching duties and preparations for his trip back to Bohemia, he only managed to complete a hundred bars. When he returned to the A flat quartet in Prague in December, he again experimented with the moment of homecoming two-thirds of the way through the movement – in the 'American' Quartet this point of recapitulation featured an opening melody transformed into something more exploratory. In this later piece Dvořák offered a more radical solution. The tune did not come back at all: instead another melody, presented early in the movement as a lyrical answer to the opening tune, assumed the function of recapitulation, the viola marked *espressivo cantabile* but in the 'wrong' key of G major. Around the viola's soulful tune the second violin wove a coquettish quintuplet rhythm – a seemingly off-the-cuff improvisation that added an extra dimension, the music conveying more than one emotion at the same time. Only at the end of the movement did the opening theme return. Compared with the earlier work, Dvořák was more daring in his juxtapositions of mood and manipulations of his opening theme to cover a wide range of emotions. Bridging Dvořák's weeks in New York and his return to Bohemia, the A flat Quartet marked his final homecoming from America: thematic transformations were the most striking feature of what would turn out to be his last chamber work.

My interest in the biographical circumstances surrounding the quartet's composition did not prevent me from suggesting to Harumi that we save ourselves some rehearsal time by changing an upcoming concert programme featuring the A flat Quartet, instead playing the 'American' Quartet that we had already performed together. Harumi took a different view: advocating Opus 105 as one of her favourite pieces, she pointed out several passages, including one in the slow movement that Dvořák composed on Christmas Day in Vysoká. After a turbulent and chromatic middle section the opening melody returned, Dvořák's heading *Tempo I e tranquillo* suggesting a satisfying recapitulation of the smooth melodic textures with which the movement began. At least that was how it seemed from the first violin part. Demisemiquavers in the second violin part were accompanied by a marking that I had not previously registered: *scherzando*. A calm melody with a joking accompaniment. Harumi drew my attention to the pizzicato quaver rhythm in the cello and viola that provided structure and buoyancy, allowing the melody to soar. The playful second-violin figurations helped the tune to encompass varied moods, at least if the first violinist was open to a changed environment: expectant yet nostalgic, innocent and aching, animated yet calm. Grateful for Harumi's enthusiasm and somewhat embarrassed by my narrow-mindedness, I agreed not to change the programme.

In August 2019, as we contemplated the precarious prospect of changing another player within the quartet, I was heartened by Harumi's fresh perspective on Opus 105. Since a string quartet's musical identity develops over time as four people work closely together, the unique sound, musical approach and relationships that result can make a group especially vulnerable to alteration. After founding violist Peter Schidlof died in 1987, the three remaining members of the thirty-nine-year-old Amadeus Quartet decided to disband, describing their late colleague as irreplaceable. And yet under the right conditions, reinventing familiar pieces with a new player can be invigorating. How successfully we accommodated a new violist would depend not only on the choice of player but on how willing the rest of us were to accommodate a lively dialogue between past interpretations and new ideas.

There is however no ideal way to manage the change of a quartet member. A gap of more than a year between founding first violinist Gábor Takács's departure and my arrival in 1993 caused uncertainty detrimental to the quartet's reputation and led to a dramatic reduction in the number of concerts we were offered. When Roger Tapping left the group in 2005, we announced his departure a year ahead of time and spent the next months auditioning players, presenting three concerts with finalists for our Boulder audience. Although input from the audience and colleagues at the University of Colorado added a dimension to the process, the potential strengths and weaknesses of a string quartet were not always easy to surmise from the outside: it was sometimes easier to gauge the potential of a new configuration in private rehearsals or around a dinner table than during a one-off concert. Our audition method combined the worst of both worlds, inviting public scrutiny without allaying uncertainty. Several concert presenters decided to delay engaging the quartet until the new violist was announced. Shortly before Geri's audition concert I retreated one afternoon to the South Boulder Recreation Center. An older man sat across from me in the hot tub staring morosely into the bubbles. 'How's your viola search coming? Roger is very good.'

After Geri announced her plans to retire, we decided to take a different approach, offering no public concerts with our viola candidates. As we began to audition several violists, I listened to our Hyperion recording with Geri of Dvořák's String Quintet in E flat, the other chamber work he had composed in Spillville. A violist himself, Dvořák expanded the voice of the instrument. The effect of his viola solos often struck me as similar to the moment that can occur during a dinner party when an unusual tone of voice causes a sudden lull in general conversation, somebody cutting through the small talk with a confession, an expression of feeling that changes the mood of the occasion. By adding a second viola in his String Quintet, Dvořák freed the first viola to assume an even greater melodic role.

After the exuberant and bustling opening music that began the second movement, a middle section in the minor key and marked at a slightly slower tempo featured one of the most glorious viola melodies in the repertoire. Geri's aptly velvet sound was familiar. Now I appreciated the variety of expressive slides she employed to reach upwards, to intensify an emphatic octave leap or as part of a diminuendo to lend vulnerability at the end of a phrase. Immediately after the highest and most expressive note, she played Dvořák's accents with desperation, even angrily for a moment, before softening her sound to end the phrase in resignation. Her expressive way of playing melodies epitomised those times when all the ties that bind the different voices of a quartet could for a moment be abandoned to the sheer pleasure of playing a great tune.

To aim for a seamless transition between departing and arriving players might be reassuring to concert presenters but I found it disconcerting to force the present and future into such close proximity, auditioning a violist on one afternoon and playing a concert the next day with Geri, as if nothing significant was taking place within the group. While we imagined our future with another violist, there was little room to acknowledge loss. In the meantime concerts continued, the audience hopefully unaware of any uneasiness within the group.

On an uncharacteristically gloomy afternoon in September 2019, I drove Richard O'Neill from his hotel in Boulder, pointing westwards as we drove down Foothills Parkway. 'You can usually see the Flatirons just over there. There are lots of trailheads just a ten-minute drive away. It's never this cloudy here. Honestly.' He laughed. 'Three hundred days of sunshine . . . really?' Since his arrival in Boulder the previous day the sun had not come out once.

Easing the first moments of our audition was the fact that we already knew Richard as a summer faculty colleague at the Music Academy of the West in Santa Barbara. Eighteen years earlier Harumi and he had played together frequently at the Marlboro Music School in Vermont, and in New York for the Chamber Music Society of Lincoln Center. Nonetheless I was nervous. To join a full-time quartet is a big commitment: a violist accustomed to a varied career of solo concerts and chamber music would need to think carefully before committing to such a move. An audition is a two-way process and the Boulder weather was not helping our cause.

Having heard Richard play with piano and as a soloist with orchestra, I was not surprised by the combination of expressive playing, momentum and crisp articulation that he brought to the *molto appassionato* viola solo in the opening *Lento* movement of Bartók's First Quartet, music in which Bartók mourned his failed love affair with violinist Stefi Geyer. If there has been an element of self-pity in the opening section that begins with a melancholy violin duet, the viola part in this new section is a cathartic outpouring that moves the music in a different direction. As Harumi joined Richard's melody, their history of playing together was apparent. Rather than choosing a safe, steady tempo, they risked the ebb and flow suggested by Bartók's *rubato* marking.

More surprising to me than Richard's assured playing was a selfless quality in the way he positioned his sound within the group, allowing space for other melodic or accompanying lines to emerge. Harumi had recently introduced me to the concept of an alley-oop in relation to string quartets. Just as a basketball player could throw the ball in such a way as to invite a teammate to jump up and slam it through the hoop, a quartet player could with a slight preparatory acceleration of tempo launch her colleague's melody, or by ending a phrase with a questioning gesture on an up-bow, invite an emphatic answer. Even in this first read-through, Richard seemed as comfortable asserting himself as he did facilitating someone else's melody. He had acquired many years of chamber music experience but this flexibility seemed to stem from a voracious curiosity that was more than just a professional attribute.

After we finished playing the exhilarating and at times raucous third movement, Richard asked about some of the more challenging passages in the other five Bartók quartets. How did we negotiate a difficult ricochet bowing that the composer had unreasonably expected us to execute at the same time as each other? What type of sound did we envisage in the whirlwind second movement of the Fourth Quartet? Richard spoke with such enthusiasm about the brain-teasing Bulgarian metre in the Fifth Quartet that I was worried he might propose reading one of the hardest movements in the repertoire. I looked at my watch. 'We should probably go if we want to keep our reservation – that restaurant gets busy.'

During dinner Richard wanted to know whether or not quartet parts had been handed down through the various changes of personnel to preserve a record of the group's bowings. Before my own audition, Gábor Takács, the founding first violinist after whom the quartet was named, had spent many hours photocopying his parts so that his successor would have easy access to the quartet's most recent markings. Although the choice of bow direction and stroke was to some extent a matter of personal taste, it saved time in first rehearsals to be able to reference the results of prior discussion and concert experience. But I was always intimidated by Gábor's markings etched in dark pencil, his charisma apparent even in the boldness of his scratched-out bowings. I purchased my own blank parts and copied in Gábor's ideas with a more cautious hand. Sometimes I tried the patience of my colleagues, my bowing ideas a contrary demonstration of independence as I tried to stamp my personality on the group.

Before founding violist Gábor Ormai died of cancer in 1995,* he had passed on all his original viola parts to Roger, many of them still encased in the black bindings

* A sad and difficult time described in my previous book *Beethoven for a Later Age: The Journey of a String Quartet.*

that Gábor Takács's father had made for the group in Budapest twenty years earlier. Gábor Ormai had a distinctive way of preparing his music, red and blue pencils used as visual aids for specific purposes. Halfway through the last movement of Bartók's First Quartet the viola enters alone with a hushed and mischievous theme that becomes a fugue, each player joining in to create a complex chatter of competing accents and rhythms. Gábor had prepared his part meticulously for this perilous passage. The blue pencil highlighted pertinent information: a reminder of the *pianissimo* at the beginning of the fugue, the first violinist's rhythm written in as a reference point just before another viola entrance. Two blue vertical lines functioned like full stops, demonstrating the end of a phrase. Red pencil was used for more critical moments, one vertical line in the middle of a note served as a warning to count the full length before moving off the note, two vertical lines as advance notice of a sudden change of dynamic. An = sign showed when a finger should be placed on more than one string at once to aid a smoother connection between consecutive notes played on different strings: as the bow moved between strings at least the left hand would already be in place.

On the same page Roger's markings had their own character, sometimes intended to avert disaster. Halfway through the fugue a dangerously quick page turn could result in the music crashing to the floor. '*Lapozz!*' Gábor had written in red pencil – turn the page! Roger reminded

himself of which hand to use: 'TURN R.H. V.S.!!' – *Volti Subito.*

After Geri joined the quartet, she preferred to use her own music, copying information across from earlier Takács parts. She had already started to assemble her parts to hand on to the next violist, a co-operative way to pass the baton during transitions that did not invariably bring out the best in people. In another quartet a departing cellist had doctored some of his music, deliberately changing bowings in order to confuse his successor. Bad behaviour was however more common among seasoned quartet players begrudging the effort of adjusting to a new player. Although my Hungarian colleagues had been kind to me, another group had welcomed their new second violinist less graciously, its cellist pausing in rehearsal to observe: 'My son, do you have any idea how beautifully your predecessor played that tune?' Another fledgling second violinist was startled by a publicity picture of her new group that included her own head Photoshopped onto the body of her predecessor, a cost-saving measure that did little to enhance her integration into the group.

Promising ourselves a celebratory photo shoot, we decided to ask Richard to be our new violist, relishing his collaborative skills, ideas, curiosity for the quartet's traditions and immediate musical bond with all of us. Enjoying the way that he and Harumi played together, András and I were ecstatic: the relationship between the inner voices of a string quartet was crucial to its well-being. We felt relieved when Richard accepted our invitation, in spite of Boulder's miserable display of weather. Due to his wish to honour existing engagements, he would not be able to join us immediately, providing us with the opportunity – so we thought at the time – to round out Geri's final season in the group by playing several Bartók cycles, returning to some of our favourite venues and programming some of her favourite pieces.

But what of our much-vaunted Central European identity? From now on a Japanese/Jewish-American and a Korean-American would be working with a British/American and one remaining Hungarian. *Gulyás* and chips would no longer suffice as a Takács meal. Already in his fifth decade as the Takács cellist, András was the tenacious thread, a vibrant melody gamely adapting to and shaping new environments as he accommodated new voices within the group.

PART TWO

Bartók's *Lontano*

To play all six Bartók quartets in two consecutive concerts is a demanding assignment that can cause unusual side-effects. Performing the final whirlwind movement of the Fourth Quartet during my first Bartók cycle in July 1995 was like being subjected to a relentless spin. I left the stage dizzy and drained, the celebratory lunch in a marquee next to Cheltenham's Pittville Pump Room marred by the large clump of hair that fell onto my Yorkshire pudding. Despite recording and performing the cycle many times since then, the experience remains stressful, and there is now less hair with which to garnish my lunch plate.

A joint project devised by the Hungarian folk music ensemble Muzsikás, founding Takács second violinist Károly Schranz and artistic consultant Joseph Horowitz helped me to approach Bartók's music with more sense of fun and adventure. In the first half of the programme we played the Fourth Quartet. Between movements the members of Muzsikás, sitting on stage behind us, stood up to play musical excerpts from regions of Eastern Europe where Bartók had conducted research trips to collect folk music. During the second half of the concert, we joined forces to play a medley of shorter pieces by

Bartók. After the members of Muzsikás played an excerpt from one of Bartók's original field recordings of a singer over loudspeakers, Károly and one of the Muzsikás violinists, Mihály Sipos, played several of Bartók's violin duos, including the one that used the same melody. When Márta Sebestyén sang the anguished 'Ballad of the Murdered Shepherd', I was entranced by the unusual accompaniment played by both Muzsikás violinists, their fast-moving bows providing an eerie shiver of barely audible sound that never grew in volume, as if the violinists were incapable of reacting to the dynamic fluctuations of the melody. The act of playing music often encouraged active co-operation but in this case the violinists' distance from the singer's expression emphasised the loneliness of her lament. For both players and audience members who found Bartók's music difficult to grasp, our joint concert provided a human context by illuminating the sources that informed his unique language early in his musical evolution.

As an ambitious young pianist and composer, Bartók was opinionated and idealistic, but he could also under the right circumstances be collaborative. In 1905 a blossoming friendship with composer Zoltán Kodály intensified Bartók's interest in folk music. Bartók was already in demand as a concert pianist, performing in the same year with the Hallé Orchestra in Manchester's Free Trade Hall, but was especially happy in Budapest as he worked with Kodály on new arrangements of twenty Hungarian folk songs for voice and piano.

The recital tour that Bartók undertook to the Iberian Peninsula in March 1906 with the thirteen-year-old violinist Ferenc Vecsey got off to a bad start. Due to a scheduling mistake, no sooner had Bartók arrived in Lisbon than he had to travel five hundred kilometres to Madrid on an 'express train' with no heating and a maximum speed of twenty-eight kilometres per hour. Even if alcohol had been more easily obtainable than it had been for Dvořák travelling through Pennsylvania thirteen years earlier, the absence of onboard lavatories during the twenty-one-hour journey would have been a deterrent. Bartók's mood was further soured two days after his twenty-sixth birthday on 25 March when he was presented to the Queen of Spain, Maria Christina of Austria, who remarked on how well Franz Joseph (Emperor of Austria and King of Hungary) spoke Hungarian. 'She talked a lot of rot,' Bartók reported to his mother, judging the whole enterprise a huge waste of time since the Queen had also failed to pay the musicians. 'If only she had known what a Habsburg-hating republican she was speaking to! Then she wouldn't have been so affable.'[1] After his concert tour with Vecsey, an at times neurotic musical partner, Bartók travelled in Portugal and Morocco before returning briefly to Spain. To avoid the kerfuffle around a royal wedding at the end of May between Alfonso XIII and Princess

Victoria Eugenie of Battenberg, he continued his journey to Venice by way of Marseille and the Milan World Exhibition. Given Bartók's early negative experiences with royalty, he might have understood the sentiment of a friend and Bartók sceptic that I was surprised to bump into outside the Sydney Conservatorium in 2011 before our Bartók cycle there. 'Anything to avoid the Royal Wedding,' he said, referring to the union of Prince William and Kate Middleton taking place in London at exactly the same time.

Towards the end of 1906, Bartók's appointment as professor of piano at the Academy of Music in Budapest enabled him to adjust the balance of his professional activities. Over the next three years he travelled less to perform concerts, concentrating instead on his teaching obligations, composition and research expeditions, an activity that he had begun a couple of years earlier with a specific goal. In preliminary studies of folk music Bartók realised that what had until then been characterised as Hungarian folk melodies were in fact more generic popular songs. From 1905 he resolved to study the issue more deeply, searching for genuine 'Hungarian peasant music'.[2] On 16 August 1907 Bartók wrote to the eighteen-year-old violinist Stefi Geyer from the Gyergyó region of Csík County in Transylvania, describing, in the form of a dialogue, his attempts to elicit authentic folk songs from a local woman. Bartók, the 'Traveller' in the dialogue, was an exacting audience, judging the singer's

first song not to be sufficiently old and the second one
even less authentic:

> Traveller: That's no good . . . It is not even old, and it's
> sung by the gentry.
> Woman: No, no! We often used to sing it in the village.
> (To her children) Now you think, too, and maybe
> you'll remember something.
> T: We don't want those that the children know. They
> are new songs. Only the very, very old ones!
> W: Where did you say you came from, sir?
> T: I've already told you, from Pest.
> W: God help ye! Are you married?
> T: No I'm not.
> W: Then you're only a youth.[3]

The encounter continued as the woman tried out various
sacred songs of no interest to Bartók, before repeating
the first tune. Eventually she suggested that Bartók visit
Gyurka Sándor's wife around the corner, who would
surely sing many old songs – especially after being
offered a drink or two. Bartók finished his letter to Geyer
complaining about the perseverance required to unearth
authentic folk music. This lively account is limited by the
fact that we hear the story only from Bartók's perspective.

Despite the minor frustrations associated with this kind
of work, between 1907 and 1936 Bartók travelled exten-
sively to study and collect songs from Hungary, Bulgaria,

Slovakia, Romania, Serbia, Turkey and North Africa. With the aid of cumbersome recording equipment that he carried with him, he was able to study and transcribe accurately the folk texts and songs that he encountered, a process that had a profound influence on his treatment of harmony and melody in his own compositions. Bartók made the liberating discovery that instead of relying on the major and minor keys that had been central to his own musical training, folk musicians employed older modes, often based on pentatonic scales. Instead of being tied to a hierarchy where within a particular key certain notes were more significant than others, Bartók envisaged a reimagining of the chromatic scale that allowed each note to be treated with equal freedom and importance.[4] In his essay 'Why and How Do We Collect Folk Music?', Bartók explained that by recording and simultaneously notating different singers' versions of the same song, researchers could most accurately analyse their melodic modifications of rhythm and pitch. The spirit of variation was most vivid when several singers were present in the same room, correcting and supplementing each other's contributions. Allowing each singer to sing more than one verse was crucial, the instinctive varying of ornaments within a melody an integral feature of their style. In this way a folk melody was like a living organism, subject to adaptation from one moment to the next.[5] Further variation could be encouraged by recording singers more than once, separating the sessions by several days. Ideally, one would return to the same village at an interval of perhaps fifteen to twenty years to record once again the same melody, hopefully now sung by both the older singers and their offspring.

Although Bartók sometimes quoted folk tunes directly in his music, particularly in his early works, more significant was the way in which he incorporated variation into his own musical language. The transformation of musical themes served also to shape entire pieces, including his string quartets. Bartók composed the Fourth Quartet, the piece that we had played for our concerts with Muzsikás, in 1928. Describing the form of the piece, he labelled the third movement as the 'kernel' around which the other movements are arranged. The first and fifth movements shared thematic material, providing the outer layer. The fourth movement was a 'free variation' on the second: together they comprised the inner layer.

When I first played the piece I found it hard to discern the connection between the frantic, nightmarish whispering of the second movement's *Prestissimo* and a humorous pizzicato fourth movement. Similarly, at first I was more aware of contrasts than connections between the outer movements. Although the piece ended with the same rhythmic declamation that concluded the first movement, the opening movement sounded uncompromising to the point of brutality, whereas the finale was an exhilarating party on the verge of getting out of control. In the centre of this symmetrical structure the cello melody that began the third movement introduced an element of humanity that seemed to spur the transformation of earlier material. A phrase that Bartók often used in describing his own work was 'free recapitulation'. As was true for the folk singers that he studied, Bartók saw the return of a melody as an opportunity for variation or transformation. For a player grappling to come to terms with Bartók's quartets, such variety could prove vexing – ingenious recapitulations full of surprises and pitfalls.

In September 2019 we travelled to Hong Kong to play our first Bartók cycle with Harumi. She blamed an involuntary eye twitch on the helter-skelter outer movements of the Fifth Quartet and the mind-boggling Bulgarian rhythm that dominated its third movement. To manage nine quavers per bar is usually an unproblematic assignment, involving a simple subdivision of 3+3+3, but Bartók groups the notes 4+2+3, an irregular metre in a fast tempo that scarcely allows a moment to blink. Just in case anyone might feel too reassured by the return of the A section (*Scherzo da capo*), Bartók occasionally slips in a new grouping: 4+3+2. Harumi's apprehension and excitement at tackling the project took me back to my first hair-raising experiences performing the cycle.

Earlier that year Harumi and I had fallen in love and started living together in Boulder. As we joined our lives together the rhythm of our relationship was – for the time being at least – shaped by our rehearsals and concert schedule. In rehearsal Harumi had a keen instinct for both leading and following. After an exchange of views within the group about a tempo, phrase shape or mood, she was adept at gauging the temperature of the room, guiding the conversation towards a good outcome. During concerts her razor-sharp focus and gutsy playing encouraged me to play freely: however daunting Bartók's complex musical language, I was grateful to tackle its challenges side by side.

According to a magazine article I read during the long flight from Denver to Hong Kong, highly effective people combatted jet lag with assertive attitude, disciplined diet and rigorous exercise routines. After executing a high-intensity intermittent training session in the hotel gym overlooking the harbour, my swollen right ankle barely fitted into a concert shoe. Struggling to keep up with the student guides who had greeted us in our hotel's lobby, I limped uphill. We passed a local diner next to a 7-Eleven, a Japanese ramen restaurant and a small McDonald's before entering a lift. After ascending one floor, to my surprise we exited into a subway underpass. A sanitised announcement echoed through the station in Cantonese, Mandarin and English. 'Due to public activities stations are subject to closure.' MTR Corporation, operator of the subway system owned largely by the city government, had become a focal point for demonstrators protesting against the erosion of democracy and the sinister, encroaching hand of the Chinese government. We had been moved to a hotel further away from the protests and urged by our concert organisers to avoid Central station and the surrounding business district. We were using Hong Kong University station's elevators, underpasses and escalators but only to take us up to the Grand Hall in the Lee Shau Kee Lecture Centre, positioned on a hill high above our hotel.

'PARENTAL ADVISORY: DON'T TRUST THE HK POLICE', read the sign pasted on a pole. On the brick plaza outside the station a student dressed in black was wearing a mask to protect himself from tear gas and facial recognition software. He stood in front of a Starbucks, its Hong Kong operation one of several Chinese-owned businesses that had become a target of protesters. We turned away from the demonstrator and the subway station and entered the concert-hall foyer. Sharon Lu, programme director of Hong Kong University's Cultural Management Office, thanked us for coming during this traumatic time: our audience would be especially small on Saturday when protests were planned. Nonetheless, she was determined to keep presenting concerts.

During our rehearsal on stage in the Grand Hall, András raised an issue in one of the supposedly easier movements that had caused disagreement between the two of us for many years. 'Inward, wistful, mumbling, passionate, desperate, reminiscing, resigned.' András described the fluctuating moods of the cello solo that began the *Non troppo lento* third movement of the Fourth

Quartet, a melody that he had been playing for nearly forty years. Chords in the violins and viola provided a rare homogeneous backdrop for a cello melody that grew in intensity through its three sections. András imagined a lament for the tragic aspects of Hungarian history, the wailing quality intensified by improvisatory flourishes that we associated with the musicians of Muzsikás. During the first phrase of the melody faster embellishments sounded like futile efforts to escape a sorrowful long note to which the cello returned. As if recalling a folk singer's alterations to a melody repeated several times, Bartók moved the cello's second phrase to a higher register, intervallic leaps that both were lyrical and emphasised the range of the cello. By its third phrase, András found the anguished leaps so extreme as to suggest a wind instrument rather than a singer.

The contentious question of dynamics arose as the melody evolved. In the second and third phrases Bartók instructed the cello to play louder but marked no corresponding increase in volume for the other parts. András's insistence that the chords maintain their quiet dynamic, while faithful to Bartók's markings, seemed to me to go against basic chamber-music instincts. Not for the first time, András reminded us of the Muszikás violinists' approach in 'Ballad of the Murdered Shepherd', their consistent low volume highlighting the isolation of the singer's melody. But in this case how natural it was to participate in the cello's increased desperation with louder and more expressive chords that otherwise might be inaudible!

The word 'rehearse' comes from the French verb *hercier*, meaning to rake or harrow. To rake over the same ground could be especially grating in the presence of an obstinate first violinist. In Hong Kong András presented a new prong to his argument. The third and most intense phrase of the cello melody had always reminded him of the toils of Sisyphus, destined to push a rock to the top of a hill, only for it at the last moment to fall to the bottom. András wished the accompaniment to convey resignation rather than toil – perhaps it occurred to him that working with a first violinist could also be a Sisyphean effort.

In my Hong Kong hotel room that night, sleepless and impatient for Benadryl to overcome jet lag – apparently not one of the strategies employed by highly effective people – I came across another aspect of Sisyphus' story described in the 'Orpheus and Eurydice' section of Ovid's *Metamorphoses*. After Orpheus' new bride Eurydice was killed by a snake bite, he turned to music to convince Hades that he should release his wife from the underworld:

> While he sang all his heart said to the sound
> of his sweet lyre, the bloodless ghosts themselves
> were weeping, and the anxious Tantalus
> stopped clutching at return-flow of the wave,
> Ixion's twisting wheel stood wonder-bound;

and Tityus' liver for a while escaped
the vultures, and the listening Belides
forgot their sieve-like bowls and even you,
O Sisyphus! sat idly on your rock![6]

Orpheus' music was so affecting that even Sisyphus inter-
rupted his hopeless task to listen. If András represented
Sisyphus toiling up the hill, perhaps the accompanying
voices had more in common with Sisyphus sitting on his
rock, transfixed by the tune.

That it had taken me twenty-six years to discover
András's idea about Sisyphus was a sign of my inade-
quacies as a listener: too often I was guilty of cutting
my colleagues off before the end of sentences to which I
thought I knew the last . . . As the timekeeper in rehearsals I was sometimes impatient in not allowing space for
new ideas to breathe. As if acknowledging the different
opinions within a group of musicians, later in the movement Bartók assigned the first violin, second violin and
viola their own variations of the cello melody, imitating
the phenomenon he had observed of four singers offering
differing versions of the same tune. In my Hong Kong
hotel room drowsiness inspired a modicum of acquies-
cence: I resolved to let people finish their sentences and
play my accompanying notes to András's melody at a
somewhat quieter volume.

As we performed the Fourth Quartet the next evening, I still had to remind myself not to get louder

beneath András's expressive tune. Part of the challenge was caused by the sudden arresting of motion after the frenetic pace of the previous movement. To generate the manic yet veiled atmosphere in the *Prestissimo* – Bartók's quiet dynamic markings exaggerated by the instruction to use mutes – was a treacherous exercise. Playing so fast and quietly, I sometimes reacted a fraction early or late to a viola or cello rhythm. I felt like a speed walker on an icy pavement: no matter how good the grips on my shoes, falling was an ever-present danger that could bring down others around me. After a previous, harried performance of the *Prestissimo*, I had hastily put my bow down on the ground beneath my music stand, anticipating the fun pizzicato movement. I had forgotten about the intervening slow movement: sheepishly recovering the bow from the ground, I tried to ignore my colleagues' ill-concealed grins. András's melody and our uneventful accompaniment required me to banish adrenalin, to acknowledge a melody more powerful in its effect if the accompaniment did not interfere. Still, I was reluctant to give up on those interesting chord progressions: I wondered how much louder I could play without András noticing.

The next morning we taxied from our Hong Kong gate at the beginning of our flight to Tokyo, a camera in the nose of the aeroplane allowing us to see the pilot's view from our seat-back television screens. At first I enjoyed the additional evidence of forward direction. But to leave Hong Kong at this fraught time in its history was to be reminded of how often the quartet's way of life could become a habit of evasion. In Hong Kong we had mothballed ourselves, turning away from the demonstrators and areas of unrest, avoiding any danger that might interfere with our ability to perform good concerts. In the meantime Hong Kongers felt deprived of a voice, exiled in their own country. Less than a year after our visit, Nathan Law, one of Hong Kong's most prominent pro-democracy student leaders, would be forced to leave his home country, fearing for his safety and dreaming of the day when he might be able to return.

As we continued to travel and perform Bartók's quartets, working on the Sixth Quartet – composed in Europe in 1939 but first performed in New York just over a year later – was an opportunity to reconsider Bartók's last years, his own exile and another musical transformation.

A photo taken in Anatolia in November 1936 shows Bartók sitting in a ramshackle wagon cluttered with luggage and equipment next to his host, the Turkish composer Ahmed Adnan Saygun. Saygun wrote a vivid account of Bartók's expedition to Turkey. After a long day listening to records in Istanbul, the two composers went for a short walk. Bartók was excited to see an unfamiliar type of fruit and wanted to know if songs existed that described the fruit. After the two men travelled to the southern city of Adana, Bartók's curiosity was piqued not only by the rustic designs of the wagons but also by the horses' bells and the different ways in which they were hitched. He could be seen running between wagons, sometimes stopping before camels to enjoy the harmonies and rhythms of their bells.

During this expedition Bartók encountered folk instruments including the zūrnā and a big drum called the davul. One evening the researchers set up their equipment in a large schoolroom lit by seven oil lamps and packed full of inquisitive villagers. Saygun recalled that when the musicians started to play, the strength with which the davul player hit his drum caused the building to shake and the lamps to flicker. Just as they seemed to be about to go out, the lamps recovered, such fluctuations of light and dark adding drama to the musicians' performances. Perhaps due to the cataclysmic

davul and penetrating zūrnā, Bartók was startled and dropped his pencil and paper to the floor, covering his ears with his hands against the vibrancy of the music surrounding him.[7] Sensitivity to loud sounds was a problem for Bartók not only during his travels. Tormented by extraneous sounds throughout his life, he had invented a white-noise machine in one Budapest apartment to mask a neighbour's radio: according to his son Péter, the ensuing din was not an improvement. Bartók was more content in the quiet neighbourhood of Buda where he lived with his family between 1932 and 1940. The rented house on Csalán út contained two pianos. Péter and Ditta – his second wife, a former student of Bartók's who performed duo concerts with her husband – were only allowed to practise when Bartók was out, practising the piano himself or (subject to negotiation) wearing earplugs. As an additional sound barrier Bartók employed a carpenter and upholsterer to build a padded door to his studio.

Although the immediacy of the zūrnā and the davul caused momentary discomfort during his trip to Anatolia, this was just the sort of experience in the field that Bartók loved. For someone often guarded in his social interactions, these research trips sparked Bartók's curiosity and enthusiasm. Over the course of the next months he and Saygun shared the wax-cylinder recordings and translations of song texts that they had collected. Saygun planned to visit Budapest to continue the joint project but just as the First World War had impeded Bartók's earlier travels, now too events intervened beyond his control.

Writing to his friend Annie Müller-Widmann from Budapest on 13 April 1938, one month after Hitler's army invaded Austria, Bartók mentioned the awful likelihood of Hungary also succumbing to 'this regime of thieves and murderers'. To stay in Hungary under such conditions was unimaginable, and yet 'to have to earn my living in some foreign country (to start toiling at the age of fifty-eight, to begin, say, teaching, and to be wholly dependent on it) would be immensely difficult and would cause me such distress of mind that I can hardly bear to think of it'.[8] Bartók's publisher Universal Edition, based in Vienna, was now under Nazi control. Along with his friend and colleague Zoltán Kodály, Bartók received a sinister questionnaire from the Viennese Society of Performing Rights that collected royalties for him, asking whether he was 'of German blood, of kindred race, or non-Aryan'. The Turkey expedition would turn out to be Bartók's last field trip to collect folk music.

In August 1939 Bartók benefitted from the generosity of the conductor and commissioner of new music Paul Sacher. After retreating to the Swiss chalet Sacher had rented in Saanen, Bartók began composing his Sixth Quartet. 'Somehow I feel like a musician of olden times – the invited guest of a patron of the arts.' The Sachers took care of Bartók's needs 'from a distance', allowing him the luxury of living and working alone 'in an ethnographic object: a genuine peasant cottage. The furnishings are not in character, but so much the better, because they are the last word in comfort. They even had a piano brought from Bern for me.'[9] Such idyllic circumstances were short-lived. Bartók returned to Budapest shortly before 1 September when Hitler's invasion of Poland commenced. The dilemma of whether or not to stay in Hungary soon reached a crisis point. Bartók completed what would turn out to be his last string quartet in November 1939. In December his mother died following a long illness, shattering one tie to Budapest. Bartók himself fell ill with what he assumed was the flu, causing a concert tour to the USA to be postponed. When the trip finally took place in April and May 1940, it paved the way for Bartók and his second wife Ditta to leave Hungary for good the following October. Péter, aged sixteen, and Béla Junior, Bartók's older son from his first marriage, remained in Budapest. 'This voyage is, actually, like plunging into the unknown from what is known but unbearable . . .'[10] Part of Bartók's uncertainty arose from poor health as he wondered for how long his constitution would allow him to work abroad. With insufficient time to process their luggage through customs at the Spanish border, the Bartóks continued their journey in their travelling clothes, leaving six heavy trunks of their belongings with customs officers to send on later. They continued their journey on the SS *Excalibur* from Lisbon to New York, arriving there on 30 October 1940.

During their first weeks in New York Bartók and Ditta lived in the cramped and noisy conditions of the Buckingham Hotel on West 57th Street, opposite Carnegie Hall. In December they moved to an apartment in the suburb of Forest Hills, Queens. Bartók wrote to his sons on Christmas Eve, contrasting festive occasions in the past with his and Ditta's loneliness in New York.

> It is bad that the post is so unreliable. Till now we have had only one letter from you, Péter (written at the end of Oct. and brought by clipper, about four weeks ago); and from you Béla, we had a postcard four days ago from Kolozsvár, dated Nov. 1st . . . It is much nicer to live here than in the centre. The streets are wide, we can also see forests, fields and lakes; there is a great deal of traffic, but it is not noisy, only the subway trains rumble every five minutes.

Despite his anxiety about the post and the difficulty of receiving an extension to his passport from the Ministry of Interior in Hungary, this was one of Bartók's most animated letters, full of detail about his new life. He and Ditta were beginning to adapt to American food, including puffed wheat, and eggs with bacon or fish for breakfast. His head was full of subway stations and street names. Reminders of home came in the form of the building's janitor, Mr Janosko, a Slovak who still spoke both Slovak and Hungarian, even after living in New York for thirty years. When Bartók was employed by Columbia University, he insulated himself in a small padded room from the disorienting cacophony of Manhattan, studying and cataloguing the Milton Parry collection of Croatian and Serbian folk songs for future publication. The support of the university temporarily brought him some financial security in his new country. His description of the ritual involved in being 'doctorated' by Columbia University was typically dry: 'Fortunately those who were being honoured did not have to say anything.'[11]

Satisfaction with the Forest Hills apartment was temporary: five months later it was judged to have been 'unsuitable in every way. It was a large apartment house, and we were piano-played and radio-blasted from right and left; a lot of noise came in from the street night and day; every five minutes we heard the rumble of the subway which made the walls shake.'[12] Perhaps Bartók and Ditta felt somewhat more settled when the six trunks of their belongings arrived in New York on 11 February 1941. By May the Bartóks had moved to Cambridge Avenue in the Bronx. For a time they were happy in their new lodgings but contentment was defined in relation to what they had left behind. The Riverdale area was peaceful and near a park with lawns, rocks and trees that reminded Bartók of the Hill of Roses in Budapest. Bartók's living conditions would however continue to be a source of anxiety for the rest of his life.

Through the gleam of brass the lettering was hard to read: 'Bartók's Retreat'. Out of habit I hung a 'Do Not Disturb' cushion over the doorknob. I was staying in the same room at the Albemarle Inn located in Asheville, North Carolina, where Bartók lived between December 1943 and April 1944, sent there by his doctors to convalesce from a condition tentatively diagnosed as tuberculosis. The ailing composer recuperated at the salubrious inn, three miles away from a bustling downtown that during the Second World War accommodated a convalescent centre for Navy officers, a command base for the US Air Force and a processing centre for refugees. Bartók regained enough strength to enjoy walking in the forests of the nearby Blue Ridge mountains. Grateful for the improvement to his health, he began collating the texts of some two thousand folk songs from the Romanian region of Wallachia. He was also busy composing a Sonata for solo violin for Yehudi Menuhin and making a piano reduction of his *Concerto for Orchestra*. Nonetheless, at times he struggled to maintain good spirits. Nearly two months before his sixty-third birthday he wrote to his friend, the Hungarian violinist József Szigeti: 'This is how I am occupied now – while awaiting the end of my exile.'[13] Bartók may have been referring to his specific situation in Asheville but never far from his thoughts was his decision to leave Hungary.

In *You Can't Go Home Again* the novelist Thomas Wolfe, born in Asheville, explored the elusive nature of home. It is unlikely that Bartók read the novel, first published posthumously in 1940, but he would have understood protagonist George Webber's sense of loss and disillusionment when Webber makes a final visit to Germany in 1936. Webber, like Wolfe, has written a book that portrays unflatteringly the residents of his home town, but it is the emergence of Hitler that brings into focus the impossibility of recapturing childhood and his optimism as a young man.

In the quiet room under the eaves the conditions should have been ideal for sleeping, but as a travelling musician I was more accustomed to carving out quiet spaces against my immediate environment. The security-door lock of a larger hotel offered reassurance from bawdy corridor voices while earplugs muted the clatter of a room-service tray delivered nearby. The silence at the Albemarle Inn was overbearing. During an unsettled night I dreamed I was walking with a cello among jostling commuters but with no case to protect it. Even knowing that the larger instrument would be crushed, I tried to squeeze it into my violin case. In Bartók's haven my restlessness was jarring, symptomatic of a life spent bouncing between airports, hotels and concert halls.

The next morning the sound of Chopin waltzes wafted through the breakfast room from a portable CD player placed discreetly behind a vase of orchids. Bartók was suspicious of radios and abhorred background music as disturbing to the fermentation of his own musical ideas. At the Albemarle Inn he tolerated communal meals, the owner at the time observing that after dinner he preferred to keep to himself, choosing to go for walks rather than linger in conversation with other guests. At least the current proprietors knew better than to select one of his string quartets as an accompaniment to eggs Benedict. Many of the faster movements would frazzle the nerves while the slow movements were eerie and questioning, ill-paired with a cappuccino gulped down in the hopes of banishing bad dreams.

The only other people at breakfast were a mother and daughter whom I presumed were visiting to enjoy the restorative benefits of the nearby mountains and early-spring flowers. After the first tubercular sanatorium opened in 1875, Asheville had become a fashionable health resort. The composer Charles Ives recuperated there in 1919 from a variety of physical ailments. F. Scott Fitzgerald featured the town at the beginning of his first novel *This Side of Paradise*, and from 1936 his wife Zelda was treated there for mental health issues.[14] But my breakfast companions were in town for a different reason, to finalise the details of a custom-made home. Built for the daughter by a local company, the house would soon be delivered to the mother's vacant lot in rural Virginia. Accustomed to squeezing in hasty visits to my parents before or after concert tours, still living in the Cambridge house I had grown up in, I envied the intimacy of this joint project between mother and daughter.

Despite the promising musical precedents established in my hotel room seventy-five years earlier, my violin practice after breakfast got off to an uninspired start. Two-thirds of the way through the second movement of the Sixth Quartet, I played a repeated pattern of two notes that began as a high shriek before plunging down through the different registers of the violin. Continuing the pattern, I leaped up the G string, an unsexy traversal of the violin's lowest string. Under my ear the violin sounded brittle and choked, a screeching squirrel in the claws of a raccoon. In Bartók's former room, the low ceiling and heavy drapes contributed to the effect. Hopefully the other Inn guests were already far away, choosing countertops and cabinets for their new house. In the breakfast room below, perhaps the chef had turned up the volume on the Chopin waltzes.

Twenty-six years ago, shortly before I moved to Boulder, I first practised this passage in my attic bedroom in Cambridge. On a balmy June afternoon my efforts mingled with the chatter of goldfinches. My mother and my brother Martin offered their own vocal imitations of the violin part, laughing as they pulled out weeds in the garden below. When my parents moved to Cambridge from Leamington Spa in 1979, the presence of an attic conversion was still unusual on Pretoria Road, a street of semi-detached and terraced houses built between 1903 and 1910 following the end of the Boer War. The room would have made a perfect study for either of them to mark essays or prepare classes but instead they earmarked it as the ideal haven for a teenager. At weekends Martin and I spread out a vivid green cloth pitch on my bedroom floor to play miniature football tournaments. We listened to the football commentaries on the radio, enjoying game updates that whisked us from blustery wind at St James' Park, Newcastle, to dreary drizzle at the Baseball Ground, Derby; from elated cacophony following a goal at Old Trafford, Manchester, to a subdued Highbury where my team Arsenal frustrated fans with another attritional display. At five o'clock every Saturday afternoon, James Alexander Gordon read out the football results, the inflections so precise that from his first syllables the outcome of each game was clear; a subdued beginning indicated the loser, an enthusiastic emphasis the victor. A pianist who had performed on cruise ships, Gordon attributed his interest in phrasing only partially to his musical studies – the false expectations created by imprecise emphasis were irksome to his father, who bet on the results. I marvelled at Gordon's concentration, never giving a result a mistaken inflection. How tempted I would have been to dash the hopes of Manchester United supporters with a deceptive: Arsenal 1 Manchester United 0!

That a small section of a Bartók quartet could trigger a happy memory of my bedroom in Cambridge did not lessen the challenge of covering such distances across the fingerboard while simultaneously trying to observe Bartók's exacting phrasing instructions. Tiny hairpins – < and > – written under each group of two notes indicated the desired emphasis: brigh-TON or FUL-ham. Bartók had called this movement *Marcia*. Although the unyielding rhythm matched the title, there was something wrong with this march. The hairpins exaggerated the effect of the rhythm – a soldier struggling to maintain balance as he lurched from one foot to the other.

Antagonism drove the music forward. At the beginning of the *Marcia* the instruments played in pairs, arguing back and forth, unwilling to march together. Individual melodies emerged to rail against the underlying rhythm. Bartók's metronome marking was a little too quick for a typical march, increasing the sense of relentless motion. Even so, I tended to choose a faster tempo than indicated. After many years of playing the piece with András, I knew how to read his concerned look in my direction at the beginning of the movement: I was tripping along, my rhythm too easy-going instead of inflexible.

In this *Marcia* Bartók seemed to evoke tyranny, even to foreshadow the horrors of concentration camps and forced marches. Growing up in Budapest under the communist system, András had experienced inflexibility and oppression in a different way. If my comfortable upbringing in Cambridge made it harder for me to inhabit the rigid character of the music, this relentless rhythm nonetheless generated its own sense of imprisonment, dictating the repetitive movements of my bow and fingers, self-expression no longer relevant. Twenty-six years after my first encounter with this music, I was holed up in an Asheville attic room still practising it. The music marched me along whether I liked it or not: no wonder I wanted to get through it as quickly as possible.

At first glance the movement was in a standard ABA form. The B section featured an anguished cello melody and an agitated rejoinder from the first violin. Where a less inventive composer would now have offered a predictable *da capo* – back to the beginning – merely repeating the *Marcia* in its previous state, Bartók transformed the opening music. The rhythm and melodic contours remained recognisable, but were now played in a soft dynamic. The second violin, viola and cello were all assigned double-stops that resulted in left hands jumping awkwardly up and down the fingerboard. Under these circumstances the quieter volume was difficult to maintain.

If I became too absorbed in the literal difficulties of managing squeaky high harmonies at the top of the group, András would urge me to sound more casual: a half-hearted soldier whistling as he continued his dreary task. Then came the passage that I practised most frequently, its crazy leaps a caricature of earlier music. In

Asheville the technical challenges of the music were only part of the reason for my continued attention. At the very moment when the music should rightfully have returned home to its opening material, I was also drawn to Bartók's distortion of the opening *Marcia*, the transformed music indifferent and nightmarish.

Bartók's childhood experience of home did not have much in common with a predictable *da capo*. The 1920 Treaty of Trianon that followed the First World War reduced Hungary's territories by around two-thirds. In 1881, the year of Bartók's birth, his home town of Nagyszentmiklós had belonged to Hungary; after the 1920 treaty it belonged to Romania. The following year Bartók wrote a short autobiographical sketch describing the many changes of home he had endured. His early years had been shaped by the loss of his father at the age of seven and his mother's struggles to support him and his younger sister Erzsébet. After his father died, 'we first went to live in Nagyszöllös (at present Czechoslovak territory), then to Beszterce in Transylvania (at present Romanian territory), and in 1893 to Poszony (Bratislava, at present Czechoslovak territory)'.[15] At least part of the reason for this last move to a town with a thriving musical life was Bartók's mother's awareness of her son's musical talent. But Bartók's insistent repetition of 'at present' in his later essay illuminated how aware he was of impermanence, of shifting boundaries within the region.

Having experienced only one childhood move from Leamington Spa to Cambridge (at present Cambridge-shire territory), I could not blame any early trauma for causing my anathema towards the traditional ABA form that occurred in a typical minuet by Haydn or Mozart. After a contrasting trio section, the opening minuet material – already heard twice thanks to the repeat signs at the ends of its two halves – was presented for yet a third time. With some notable exceptions it seemed to me that composers hastily tossed off their minuets, conserving their creative energies for the grander chal-lenges of a finale. Admittedly, my impatience with the minuet as a form betrayed a lack of appreciation for its original function as a dance. A clumsy dancer myself, the joyful return of a familiar step was lost on me – merely further confirmation of incompetence. I preferred those composers who used traditional musical forms to create the expectation of return, only for the off-balance soldier to take one in a different direction. No one did it better than Bartók.

In the peaceful environment of the Albemarle Inn Bartók regained strength and put on some weight, at least by his standards. On 30 January 1944 he wrote to Szigeti: 'In March my weight was 87 lbs., now it is 105 lbs. I am getting stout. Too stout. As stout as anything.'[16] When his son Péter visited him later in the spring, he noticed his father's fascination with the birds that sang every morning outside the bedroom window. Bartók pointed out to Péter the bird whose call ended differently each time, with fewer or more notes. He wrote down transcriptions of the birdsong he heard in a black notebook, a reminder of happier times as a younger man spent in the field collecting folk music. The worsening situation in Hungary continued to distress Bartók. When he and Ditta left Hungary they had hoped that it would not be an irreversible journey. In June 1941 they still held out hopes of returning there: 'If things are bad everywhere, one prefers to be at home.'[17] Accustomed to a modicum of fame and success in Hungary, Bartók's financial hardship and reliance on the generosity of others to help with his medical expenses exacerbated a sense of being unmoored in America. But by July 1945 Bartók was more resigned to his new domicile. He wrote to his friend Jenö Zádor from upstate New York that news of devastation, misery and chaos from Hungary was extremely dispiriting: even though he still wished for the possibility of returning there permanently, he could no longer seriously consider it. Bartók made a brief trip over the border to Montreal to renew the necessary visa for his continued residence in the USA.

To be nearer to his doctors, early in September 1945 he returned with Ditta and Péter from upstate New York to Manhattan. With heartless pedantry their landlord advised that the presence of Péter staying in their two-room apartment on West 57th Street constituted a breach of contract: the wear to the rug of three people walking on it was not covered by their rent. As Bartók's health continued to deteriorate the landlord sent his agent to Bartók's bedside to inform him that his lease would not be renewed at the end of the month. But before Bartók could begin searching for new lodgings, his doctors insisted that he be moved to the West Side Hospital, omitting from their communication that there was nothing further they could do to prolong his life. Bartók died in hospital on 26 September 1945 from complications arising from leukaemia. His funeral was held at the Universal Chapel on Lexington Avenue. Bartók was buried in the Ferncliff Cemetery in Hartsdale, Westchester County, with between twenty and thirty people in attendance.

The journey of Bartók's Sixth Quartet from Hungary to New York paralleled that of its composer. In the idyllic setting of Sacher's Swiss chalet, Bartók probably imagined that the first performance would take place in Budapest or elsewhere in Europe. The work had been intended for the Hungarian String Quartet but the group remained in Amsterdam during the Second World War, making communication between the players and composer difficult. The piece was eventually dedicated to the Kolisch Quartet, who gave the world premiere on 20 January 1941 in New York City's Town Hall – the same day that Franklin Roosevelt was inaugurated for his third term. In the 'Amusements' section of the *New York*

Times, above a striking advertisement for rumba classes, reviewer Howard Taubman observed a characteristic in the new work, 'not a radiant, natural simplicity, but a simplicity that comes from rigorous, intellectual discipline'.[18] It is doubtful that simplicity was the word uppermost in the players' or audience's mind during the premiere. The rigour of the inexorable *Marcia* rhythm accompanied Bartók's last years in America, a weary traveller forced to move between rented lodgings and rural retreats as his leukaemia advanced.

In 1988, at the request of his sons Péter and Béla Junior, Bartók's remains were returned to Budapest for a state funeral. The coffin was transported across the Atlantic on the *Queen Elizabeth 2*, its journey marked by memorial concerts in Southampton, Cherbourg, Paris, Strasbourg, Munich and Vienna. This time there was no danger of any luggage getting lost. Bartók's coffin was reburied in a single grave with Ditta, his mother and his mother's sister, at the Farkasréti Cemetery on the Buda side of the Danube.

The bleak circumstances of Bartók's departure from Hungary and last years in America were on my mind when the Takács made the journey back to Budapest from Denver in November 2019 to perform his Sixth Quartet at the Franz Liszt Academy of Music: the quartet's spiritual home, where its original members had first formed as students. But any meditations on the resonance of such a voyage were quickly pushed to one side by the vagaries of airline travel. Shortly after the Dreamliner was pushed back from the gate we felt the judder of an impact. The tug had bumped into the plane's nose gear. While we waited for several hours for the maintenance team to assess the damage, the standard United Airlines script thanking us for our patience did not appeal to our captain: 'It's a screw-up: I don't know what else to say.'

Fifteen hours later I handed our boarding passes across the desk to a laconic Lufthansa employee. Although two conveniently direct flights to Budapest showed on the departures screen above the Lufthansa desk, our revised schedule on Austrian Airlines included an extra plane change in Vienna and a short connection time. Delayed flights and missed connections exposed the limits of the much-vaunted Star Alliance, a rhetoric of collaboration that when push came to shove rarely delivered satisfactory results. That my frustration seemed shamefully self-indulgent, in the context of Bartók and Ditta's separation from most of their belongings during their arduous journey into the unknown, did nothing to improve my spirits. When I hit my head on a table after bending down to retrieve a fork, Harumi knew better than to thank me for my patience.

The unpredictability of travel setbacks has never discouraged me from fleshing out concrete details of future catastrophes. By the time we boarded a tiny plane for our last flight to Budapest there would be no space for our violins in the shallow overhead bins, we would be denied boarding, and the four-hour train journey would only be possible the following morning, our subsequent rehearsal marred by a fractious first violinist, the jet-lagged concert in the spiritual home of the quartet resulting in no re-engagement. But as we boarded our flight to Vienna, Austrian Airlines' welcome music compilation of Johann Strauss waltzes sounded at a lower volume than usual, providing welcome contrast to United's Gershwin-infused safety video. When an agent dressed in a red three-piece suit approached us at the gate in Vienna with checked-bag labels, I braced for a tense debate about the impossibility of stowing fragile Italian instruments in the hold. Instead he proceeded merely to tag all the nearby rollaboard suitcases. Bright red suits were suddenly magnificent and Austrian Airlines the best airline in the world, a crucial cog in a glorious alliance of international co-operation. Our turboprop plane retained the romance of early plane travel so lamentably lacking in contemporary designs – and required no tugging. In Budapest we were reunited with suitcases, now adorned with new Lufthansa baggage tags: FRA–BUD – they at least had been deemed worthy of a direct flight.

The next afternoon András led us from the hotel to our rehearsal at the Franz Liszt Academy, the same building where Bartók had taught between 1907 and 1939. András had arrived several days before us in order to spend time with his ailing mother, who for the first time since I had joined the quartet would be unable to attend our concert at the Franz Liszt Academy. As the sole remaining Hungarian in the group, András seemed to feel added responsibility, guiding us along scenic side streets, apologising for the weather and urging us to explore the historic part of town closer to the Parliament buildings.

When I asked András if he ever felt homesick for Budapest, he answered that he missed walking on the streets between Vörösmarty Square and the Great Market Square. He missed the possibility of more regular visits to relatives, old friends and professors from the Franz Liszt Academy:

> I felt the most alone a couple of years after we left,
> not in Boulder but when I came back to Budapest. I
> walked to my favourite place by the Danube opposite
> the Royal Palace and Chain Bridge, where I used to love
> the feeling of being enveloped in the scent and history
> of the river. I felt like an outsider who just happened to
> speak the language fairly well – maybe it was just bad
> luck that my friends happened to be out of town, but
> also all those quartet rehearsals and concerts made it
> harder to stay in touch. Now I miss the warm, round-
> the-table conversations and especially that type of
> cynical humour that comes from our painful history. In
> a way communism united us: the idea that with it gone

everything would be fine turned out to be a myth. Now who is there to blame for our problems?

Despite his reservations about returning to Budapest, András seemed younger, more buoyant, walking on the streets where he had been a student. To recall student days, however, was not always a liberating experience. The first time I came to Hungary in September 1996 with the Takács, we spent a week rehearsing and performing Bartók's First, Third and Fifth Quartets in preparation for a recording session. I was daunted by the prospect of performing in the city where the group had been formed until I observed the wan faces of Károly and András in our green room. Before our concert a steady procession of professors entered to greet their former pupils. To return home as successful professionals was only a part of the story: playing for former teachers was also to be reminded of past deferential selves. From the VIP boxes high above the stage, the president and professors of the Academy looked down on us during the concert. In New York or London I might experience similar regressions, but that evening in the presence of my nervous Hungarian colleagues I felt unencumbered, grateful for the lack of any past associations.

During subsequent short visits to Budapest to play concerts, I had not made the effort to explore any of the neighbourhoods where Bartók lived, but now I was curious to visit the house where he had spent his last years in Hungary – 'in nearly ideal circumstances', according to Péter. This was the same home where he significantly changed the ending of the Sixth Quartet, completing in November 1939 the piece that he had begun the previous summer in the Swiss Alps. Perhaps in this happier home environment with its padded studio and strict rules about family practising, I would find evidence of a more energetic Bartók than the man who just a few years later would be struggling to regain his health in Asheville, North Carolina.

Bartók would have approved of the security measures in place outside 29 Csalán Way: only after explaining our purpose into the speakerphone next to a white diamond-mesh gate were Harumi and I allowed access to a garden that sloped upwards towards the house. Screened by trees and shrubs, the Bartók Béla Emlékház (Memorial House) was set far back from the street. Near the house, facing away from approaching visitors, Imre Varga's sculpture of Bartók was meticulously dressed in a shirt and tie, jacket buttoned shut and hands thrust deep into overcoat pockets. The gaunt ascetic stared out into the distance, seeming to discourage the approach of any visitors who might wish to pose for a selfie.

Anxious to start the tour, I was oblivious to the wishes of the woman who greeted us in the hallway, Harumi more alert to her repeated beckoning towards the cloak-room – an indication that we should leave our coats there.

Before our guide was able to explain that taking photographs was forbidden, Harumi had snapped a picture on the wall: 'All my life, in every sphere, always and in every way, I shall have one objective: the good of Hungary and the Hungarian nation.'[19] On 8 September 1903, four months after graduating from the Franz Liszt Academy, Bartók had written to his mother from the resort town of Gmunden in Austria. Consistent with his nationalist views at the time, this frequently quoted sentence was a prelude to Bartók scolding her for not speaking Hungarian more consistently. From a young age his mother had spoken German with her sister but Bartók felt ashamed when she slipped into it on other occasions. 'Speak in a foreign language only when absolutely necessary!'

By 1931 Bartók would still have encouraged his family to speak Hungarian whenever possible, but his nationalist perspective had changed. To the best of his abilities he wished his music to serve the idea of 'the brotherhood of peoples, brotherhood in spite of wars and conflicts'.[20] In 1942 he wrote an essay entitled 'Race Purity in Music' for the New York publication *Modern Music*, in which he reflected on the universal language of folk music. He described the cross-pollination of melodies as they migrated back and forth between regions: 'A Hungarian melody is taken over, let's say by the Slovakians and "Slovakised"; this Slovakised form may then be retaken by the Hungarians and so "re-magyarised". But – and again I say fortunately – this new form will be different

149

from the original Hungarian.'[21] The early nationalist quote that greeted us in the hallway of the Memorial House was unrepresentative of the internationalist that Bartók later became.

Our guide began by describing the house as the last place that Bartók had lived before leaving Hungary for ever. Nonplussed by my frequent interruptions, intended to demonstrate my knowledge of the subject, she explained the topographical map of the Carpathian mountains at the bottom of the stairs that, when you pressed on a button, highlighted the different villages where Bartók had collected folk music. 'It's a fine line between expressing enthusiasm and interrupting,' Harumi would later comment with a smile, not needing to clarify which side of the line I had crossed.

Bartók would have liked our guide, who approached her assignment with quiet earnestness, as if wishing not to disturb the composer still revising his Sixth String Quartet in the studio above. As she led us upstairs, I realised that there would be no licence to roam freely through the house. Sweltering in the coat I had refused to relinquish, I asked if she thought Hungarians today liked Bartók's music. Did she play an instrument? Considering that our guide showed as much interest in small talk as Bartók, she made a gracious effort to engage, saying that many people still found Bartók's music very modern and that as a young child she had enjoyed playing some of his piano pieces for children.

Bartók's music studio was no longer separated from the main room on the second floor. The adjoining wall and padded door had been knocked out to facilitate visitors viewing a cramped space that included Bartók's Bösendorfer piano and some of the recording equipment he had lugged around on his travels. Bartók often smoked while composing at this piano. When the Bösendorfer was restored as part of a major renovation of the house, the piano technician found an ancient butt inside the frame, apparently from Bartók's favourite brand of cigarettes.

In the larger room next to the music studio on the second floor, our guide pointed out several pieces of furniture made in a folk style by the carpenter György Gyugyi Péntek, from whom Bartók had first ordered a writing desk during his trip to Transylvania in the summer of 1907. Two photographs on the walls showed different character traits than Varga's sculpture. In the first Bartók enfolded his second wife Ditta in a tight hug; in the other he leaned casually against a wooden dresser decorated with floral engravings. I was surprised by Bartók's seemingly carefree demeanour, enhanced by bare toes that protruded from his sandals. Our guide became animated: 'He is that way because Ditta took the picture – they were very much in love.' Near the wooden furniture a collection of colourful jugs in the living area reminded me of a story told by Péter that showed a more playful side of his father. Two water pitchers had been designed to frustrate attempts to pour from them: concealed openings near the necks caused the liquid to spill, an effective prop with which to prank visitors.

Up another flight of stairs an attic had been converted into an airy, light-filled museum space. Before I could offer a dubious theory of my own, Harumi asked the guide about an unusually large ticket in one of the display cases. This was Péter's project – a joke award to his father that he had typed out, complimenting him on the achievement of obtaining Thomas Mann's signature. Behind the parody of a child perhaps bored by his father's many awards lay a sinister political backdrop. When the Committee for Literature and Art of the League of Nations met in Budapest on 8 June 1936, several artists on the committee refused to attend a government reception that would have necessitated sitting at the same table as the Hungarian Minister of Culture, Bálint Hóman, a pro-Nazi politician responsible for the laws that persecuted Jews in Hungary throughout the 1930s and 1940s. Instead Bartók spent the evening with Thomas Mann.

Although painstaking efforts had been made to recapture a sense of Bartók's living quarters, many aspects of the exhibition drew attention to the fact that what mattered to him most lay elsewhere: the model of the Carpathian mountains, or the dried insects pierced with needles and mounted in a glass case, which highlighted Bartók's lifelong fascination with the natural world.

In the house where Bartók had felt most at home, the silence that honoured his aversion to background music accentuated the gloom. The cigarette butt, Péntek's imaginative furniture, the phonograph player and insect collection were vivid details that served to emphasise absence. Even Péter's story about the jugs designed to trick visitors was tinged by the regret that his parents received so few visitors, not all of whom were suitable subjects for such jests. The Memorial House was aptly named. As we left the garden I noticed a sandpit in a small playground opposite the entrance gate. On a grey November morning the yellow lorry lying on its side, next to a mud-spattered bucket and a partially submerged spade, suggested departed children more than recent play. The sandpit reminded me of my American grandmother's house in Manchester, New Hampshire, where I stayed for several months when I was three years old. I must have spent many joyful hours grubbing around in her sandpit, but I remembered it as a place to wave goodbye and await my parents' return from their research projects in Boston. That I had hoped for a more invigorating experience at the Memorial House was a reminder of how often the expectation of a particular emotional effect could be confounded, by a house as much as a piece of music. But as Harumi and I crossed the river back to our hotel to rest before our concert, I was grateful to be able to imagine Bartók at his Bösendorfer piano in November 1939, his plans for a lively conclusion to the Sixth Quartet about to undergo a radical change.

My music was open on the stand but at the beginning I could only listen. A string quartet was usually a collaborative project but for nearly a whole minute Geri played the tune alone: *Mesto* – sad. At first I felt as if I was eavesdropping on a private sorrow, but as the melody climbed higher the viola became declamatory, as if conscious of an audience. I could not evade the sad mood.

The initial outpouring dissipated and the melody faded away. Silence. Rudely we shattered the sombre mood, playing the same loud notes and rhythm as each other – vigorous bow-strokes that banished the melancholy. No more sadness then. After another pause we exchanged hushed flurries of notes back and forth, the quietly bustling energy of the subsequent music offering a more sustained rejoinder to the opening tune: the slow introduction satisfactorily dismissed by faster music. At the end of the movement came a solo of a different nature. After I ascended to a high note the others resolved beneath me onto a sweet major chord. I was left playing alone, the effect peaceful, ethereal.

Mesto: our cellist András played the same viola melody that opened the Sixth Quartet – not so easily dismissed, after all. At the beginning of the second movement I enjoyed the contradiction between the insistent sadness and the reassuring repetition of this beautiful tune.

Joining in with a counter-melody I was shadowed by the second violin and viola, who played the same notes with a tremolo bow-stroke: an accompaniment that surrounded the tune with an eerie shiver. As the cello melody became more impassioned, so too did the accompaniment. Although not yet equal participants, we were now helping to create the mood.

Again the melody faded to silence. At least that is how it is supposed to be: a sneeze exploded and echoed in the hall. Harumi waited a little longer than usual before playing her next four notes: an acknowledgement that within this piece silence had an important role to play, preceding many pivotal changes of mood. After the forceful *Marcia* that I practised in Asheville, again the *Mesto* melody began the third movement. I began alone but immediately the second violin and cello joined with the same *mezzo forte* dynamics, now equal participants: what had begun as a lonely utterance in the solo viola had become more co-operative in this third movement. Geri listened to the three of us: a mirror image of the opening of the piece, where we had listened to her solo. Later she joined the melody as it grew in intensity. Exhausting itself, the music faded to silence.

For the quartet player, musical opportunities to revel in rudeness are scarce, but the section near the beginning of the *Burletta* provides one of the most striking: the second violin hammering out a repeated quaver rhythm – a jagged theme that ends with a slimy glissando, one pitch sliding into the next. Bartók added the first violin to the slide but a quarter-tone lower – a dissonant and sarcastic sneer. After so many hours spent trying to make beautiful sounds and play in tune with each other, it was liberating to sound ugly, aggressively humorous – clowns entering to lampoon the tragic mood. Comic relief was welcome but to laugh was to let down one's guard. Increasingly Bartók made the joke at our expense. As the *Burletta* unfolded the humour became more and more grotesque. Over the course of the first three movements the reactions to the *Mesto* had become more extreme, increasingly desperate attempts to escape the sadness. And yet this apparent dichotomy did not tell the whole story. To craft his musical themes for the first three movements, Bartók in fact drew on material from the very same *Mesto*, transforming its melodic shapes to create sharply contrasting music. The clowns might rail against a particular emotion, seek to brush it to one side, but our extreme reaction would turn out to be no match for the slow music.

Mesto: at the beginning of the fourth and final movement I began the melody once again, but for the first time the initial sound came not from a solo instrument but from first violin, second violin and viola, the cello joining in before I could finish my phrase – a lonely melody turned into a shared sorrow. At first Bartók had intended this fourth version of the *Mesto* merely as a slow introduction to a faster movement. In the final version, however, composed in November 1939, the *Mesto* expanded to take over the final movement, displacing Bartók's original plans for a livelier ending. The four voices, so often in conflict in previous movements, commented on and intensified each other's gestures, the communication of emotion unified.

At the very moment that Bartók had originally planned a fast movement, a brief setting of the *Mesto* melody as a kind of chorale was followed by the return of the two major themes from the first movement, devoid of vigour and momentum. Harumi and Geri recalled a tune that towards the end of the first movement had assumed a dance-like swagger, but was here transformed by the slower tempo and Bartók's instructions to the players: *Più dolce, lontano* – more sweetly, at a distance. They moved their bows closer to the fingerboard to create a more fragile sound. By assigning the tune to the middle voices in the quartet, Bartók avoided the more extreme registers of first violin and cello, increasing the sense of remoteness. *Lontano*: the music to be experienced at a distance – an idea that Bartók imagined against a background of advancing chaos and horror. Whether in a secluded Alpine chalet or his insulated music studio at Csalán Way, Bartók sought to protect his musical ideas from the terrifying din of the outside world. The sweet *lontano* melody heard at such a distance as to be almost out of reach could be experienced as the saddest place in the whole piece. And yet whenever we played this passage, what I loved was not the sense of distance but the closeness between second violin and viola. Bartók placed the viola a sixth lower than the violin – the way the players traversed these harmonious intervals together was for those of us in the midst of the performance an experience of innermost communication. After the dissonance, sarcasm and relentless rhythm that dominated the middle movements of the quartet, this music contained a kernel of hope, the possibility of redemption.

At the end of the piece, Geri played the first phrase of the opening melody for the last time. Repeating the melodic shape of the first five notes, András answered with pizzicato chords, the upward gesture, consonant harmonies and *diminuendo* not exactly hopeful, but posing a question as to what the future might bring.

In Bartók's mind the creation of his Sixth Quartet came at a great cost. On 2 April 1940, three and a half months after his mother's death, he expressed regret that he had not done more to make her last years easier. In Saanen he had composed the *Divertimento* for strings and most of the Sixth Quartet, but 'those three and a half weeks I took away from my mother. I can never make amends for this. I should not have done it – and there were many similar things in the past – and none of this can be helped now.'[22]

In their own ways both my parents were responsible for introducing me to a play that in its emotional range reminded me of Bartók's Sixth Quartet. My mother was a Shakespearean scholar whose enthusiasm for live theatre went hand in hand with her ability to provoke discussion around the kitchen table after we attended open-air Shakespeare productions by undergraduate students. My father first drew my attention to his favourite scene in *King Lear*. In Act IV, scene vii, the King's doctor reassures Cordelia that after her father's fits of madness, Lear will awaken recovered. The stage direction calls for music, believed by the Elizabethans to restore sanity. As the doctor urges Cordelia to approach her father, he instructs the musicians: 'Louder the music there.' When Lear awakens he thinks he has died, but he slowly recognises his daughter and asks her forgiveness, acknowledging that he is a foolish old man. As a teenager I used to challenge what I judged to be my father's disproportionate highlighting of such positive moments, even in the bleakest of films or plays. Later I saw his penchant for seeking out such glimmers of humanity in the context of his profession as an American historian, who for over thirty years immersed himself in the horrors of slavery.[23] Although my father focused on this one scene, in the midst of cruelty and brutality Cordelia provided a thread of goodness throughout the play.

In the context of the whole piece, Bartók's *lontano* seemed to offer some hope of restored sanity. Bartók had allowed the recurring *Mesto* to disturb his original conception for the piece and in so doing created a space for this duet, a duet that could not have emerged from the busy first movement, alien march or grotesque burlesque.

Through his *lontano* instruction to the players, Bartók realised the opposite musical experience to the piercing cry of the zūrnā that he had plugged his ears against in Anatolia in 1936, the shattering blows of the davul that caused candles to flicker and windows to shake. As I accompanied the *lontano* melody on the same stage where Bartók had performed his final concert with Ditta before leaving Hungary, Harumi and Geri's scarcely audible duet transcended any particular place or time, emerging from sadness to offer the hope of co-operation, both immediate and out of reach.

Where Britten Belongs?

'If I say the loudspeaker is the principal enemy of music, I don't mean that I am not grateful to it as a means of education or study, or as an evoker of memories. But it is not part of true musical *experience*.' So Benjamin Britten pronounced to his audience at the Aspen Amphitheatre on 31 July 1964 after he had travelled to Colorado to receive the first Aspen Award for Services to the Humanities from the Aspen Institute. Music 'demands some preparation, some effort, a journey to a special place, saving up for a ticket, some homework on the programme perhaps, some clarification of the ears and sharpening of the instincts. It demands as much effort on the listener's part as the two other corners of the triangle, this holy triangle of composer, performer and listener.'[1]

One afternoon in April 2020, Britten would not have been impressed by my contribution to the holy triangle. No ticket saved up for, no journey undertaken: in the house that Harumi and I had rented in Boulder, some two hundred miles east of Aspen, I grabbed my phone, a pair of headphones and a miniature score, opened the sliding door of the kitchen and padded twenty feet to the wooden deck at the back of the house that faced west towards the mountains.

COVID-19 had thrown Harumi and me into even closer proximity, our concerts and recordings cancelled for at least the next several months. We were fortunate to have rented a house large enough to accommodate separate practice studios. Nonetheless, the ups and downs of quartet life could be amplified when two people experienced them concurrently. Each morning I sat at the dining table hunched over my cellphone, muttering glumly about the prospects of a string quartet with no upcoming live concerts and a new violist stranded in California. One of Harumi's favourite coronavirus cartoons featured a man sitting on a couch next to a large rock and the caption: 'Sisyphus Works From Home.'

In recent days the indiscriminate roar of traffic on Foothills Parkway had been replaced by more distinct sounds: a truck grinding down through gears and the impulsive zoom of a motorcycle competing with the siren of an ambulance arriving at the nearby hospital. Gusts of wind provoked the chimes left behind by previous occupants and melted snow gushed through the rain gutters. From adjacent trees two black-capped chickadees whistled their distinctive song, the first of the two-note pattern always higher: F sharp–E answered by G–E. The E pitch was enviably consistent between the two birds and the timing of the calls apparently respectful. Knowing nothing about chickadees I heard a well-tuned and co-operative conversation, perhaps a courting ritual. A Google search revealed my ignorance: these were in fact two males competing for a mate, their rivalry more obvious when their fee-bee calls coincided, G clashing against F sharp, just a semitone below. Now the call seemed more insistent, the piercing tone and projection impressive from such a small bird. For males whose only distinguishing visual characteristic was a somewhat larger black bib than the females', this was a vocal duel of reproductive significance.

Under these circumstances Britten might have conceded the benefits of noise-cancelling headphones, blocking out intrusive sounds as I began to listen to his String Quartet in D major, Opus 25. Britten had started composing music for string quartet as a child and continued to develop his interest in the genre during his student days at the Royal College of Music. He composed this four-movement work in California during the summer of 1941 when he was twenty-seven years old, the first effort in the genre that he deemed worthy of an opus number.

As a listener I was better able to appreciate the ecstatic yet serene atmosphere of the opening than when we had recorded the piece in 2013 for the centenary of Britten's birth, the violins and viola playing high notes that shimmered above cello *pizzicati*. Less preoccupied by the problem of tuning notes sometimes only a semitone apart from the second violin, I was astounded by the cello part. What was András doing so many octaves below the three of us? Even on the page of my score the visual effect of his *pizzicati* was strikingly independent from our notes perched on leger lines high above the stave. And yet the chords that András's notes traced out gave our ethereal wanderings a harmonic foundation. Continuing his *pizzicati*, András reached upwards to a high note. Through headphones the gesture struck me as more co-operative than it did in person, as if András was inspired by the altitude of his colleagues. A combination of independence and collaboration typified his role in the Takács. Over the course of forty-five years he had become expert at balancing the demands of the quartet with the regularity of family dinners, tennis games and time in his vegetable garden. We had not travelled together for several weeks and I already missed his judicious sense of timing, sidling up to the gate in the early morning only as boarding was announced, and in so doing avoiding the sleep-deprived banalities of his colleagues.

When we recorded the piece I had enjoyed the challenge of Britten's sudden and frequent changes of tempo, the way that the radiant opening music faded away to be replaced by an *Allegro vivo* – energetic, syncopated and as sure of itself as the previous phrases were exploratory. In relation to the opening, this new music was a no-nonsense rejoinder: a mother who took her child's hand and strode forward, impatient with his reveries. Listening outside on the deck, I was unsettled by fractured music that could not make up its mind whether it was fast or slow. Britten was only partially to blame for my unease, increased by an injudicious intake of caffeine and sugar – an attempted buffer against grim news of daily COVID death tolls and the suspended state in which I found myself. When hushed, scurrying rhythms dissolved once more into the opening slow tempo, the violins and viola playing even higher while András stubbornly resumed his *pizzicati*, I distrusted this return of the slow music: an exploratory interlude that was provisional, subject to change. Vacillation between the two tempi became more frequent towards the end of the movement. The *Allegro vivo* had the last say: this time a skeletal version of the syncopated rhythm was played pizzicato by all the instruments, the other parts conceding to the cello's earlier mutiny.

'To Mrs Elizabeth Coolidge', the dedication read at the top of my Britten score. Perhaps Britten should have expanded his holy triangle to acknowledge the crucial role of patrons in the genesis of a musical composition. Elizabeth Sprague Coolidge was the most significant supporter of chamber music in the USA in the first half of the twentieth century. In 1940 she commissioned Britten to compose a string quartet, a piece that he had already been planning to write for an English-based ensemble, the Griller Quartet. After the group's proposed tour to the USA in 1940–1 was cancelled, Coolidge provided fresh impetus for the project. Britten would complete the work in California in the summer of 1941 under unusual circumstances.

The first performances were assigned to the Coolidge Quartet, a group that had apparently suffered some interpersonal problems. When the violist Nicolas Moldovan complained to his patron about the first violinist, Coolidge replied: 'I consider William Kroll as the leader of the quartet, and must leave it to you both to decide whether you wish to play together. To me it is a matter of indifference. Please do not reopen this useless discussion.'[2] Perhaps Kroll took his patron's endorsement too much to heart: by the time the Coolidge Quartet worked with Britten, David Dawson had become their new violist. While this was the group's only change of violist, Kroll presided over a remarkable turnover of five second violinists and three cellists during the eight-year lifespan of the ensemble. I listened to excerpts of the group's recording of Hindemith's String Quartet no. 4, Opus 22, that began with first violin alone, followed by the viola playing the same theme. Kroll might have reduced his volume a touch more to draw the ear to Moldovan's melodic line, but I found it hard to discern from his playing what might have made him such a difficult colleague. Nonetheless, in 1944 the Coolidge Quartet disbanded and Kroll formed a new string quartet called – perhaps unsurprisingly – the Kroll Quartet.

I envied the possibility of any quartet interaction, however fraught. Our last concert with Geri had been in early March at the University of Colorado, her retirement from the group accelerated by two months, following the cancellation of all concerts. Now we awaited Richard's arrival in June, wondering what projects if any would remain to shape our first rehearsal period together.

In May 1939 the twenty-five-year-old Britten crossed the Atlantic with his friend, the tenor Peter Pears, on the RMS *Ausonia*. 'The boat's not too bad – except that there's nothing to do,' Britten wrote to Wulff Scherchen, until recently his lover. 'It's so bloody boring. Eat, sleep, ping-pong, eat, walk, decks, eat, eat, deck-tennis, eat, read, sleep – etc. ad infinitum.'[3] The good company of Pears at least compensated for the 'fearfully boring crowd of English bourgeoisie on holiday'. Britten enjoyed reading *1066 and All That*, the classic satirical history of England, one of whose authors, R. J. Yeatman, was on board the ship. The tedium was perhaps not altogether unwelcome, as the journey enabled Britten to extricate himself from a complicated romantic situation he had handled badly. Scherchen had only found out about Britten and Pears's plans to leave England at a farewell party he stumbled upon at their London flat in mid-April. He spent the evening getting drunk and sobbing in a corner until Britten accompanied him by taxi to the nearest train station.[4]

Britten's inability to focus on any serious reading or composing was shortly compounded by the 'unadulterated misery' of a ferocious gale: 'The ship bumps, pitches & rolls which makes moving about & keeping still equally

unpleasant.' To Scherchen Britten expressed his homesickness for the old mill he had purchased in 1937 near
Aldeburgh on the Suffolk coast: 'What a fool one is to
come away – the more I think of Snape [. . .] the more I
feel a fool to have left it all.' But his regret did not convey
the whole story. Britten had overseen the conversion of
the mill into idiosyncratic living quarters that he shared
with a lodger, the composer Lennox Berkeley. According
to Britten, Berkeley had hoped for a more intimate relationship – another complication that Britten was relieved
to escape. He wrote to Berkeley from the ship, ending the
letter with the cloying concern of a guilty runaway: 'I do
hope that you're feeling O.K. my dear. I think about you a
great deal – really!'[5] Several months later Britten would
ask Berkeley to give Scherchen some money Britten
owed him, promising to repay Berkeley at a later date,
the neatness of the arrangement more convenient for the
debtor than those he had left behind.

Surrounded by icebergs, Britten wrote to his friend
Aaron Copland that 'a thousand reasons – mostly problems' had prompted his departure from England.[6] As
early as 1930 Britten had complained in his diary that
his composition teacher Frank Bridge enjoyed more recognition in America than in his own country. Bridge was
an earlier beneficiary of Elizabeth Sprague Coolidge's
patronage and had recommended his talented pupil to
her. The possibility of professional opportunities was
again on Britten's mind in 1937 when he wrote to Pears,

envying his friend's upcoming tour to America and resolving that he must go there himself before too long. The appeal of America complemented Britten's growing disillusionment with England. In April 1935, two years after his graduation from the Royal College of Music, Britten had been approached by the General Post Office whose new public relations officer, Sir Stephen Tallents, had brought with him several documentary film-makers from his previous position at the Empire Marketing Board. Under the guise of making short marketing videos for the GPO, this team saw an opportunity to distribute their revealing exposés of working-class life to a wider audience. The GPO's new Film Unit hired Britten to be their resident composer. During the next four years he learned how to harness his imagination to the needs of directors and scripts, and to compose on demand even when feeling uninspired. It was here that Britten met the iconoclastic writer W. H. Auden. They collaborated on several films including *Coal Face*, a vivid portrayal of the everyday dangers endured by miners, and *Night Mail*, a twenty-four-minute documentary about postal workers working on the overnight express-mail train from London to Scotland. Auden's forceful personality and left-wing views contributed to Britten's dissatisfaction with both the British Establishment and the state of Europe.

In 1959 Britten would look back critically on his own attitudes during the grim period following Neville Chamberlain's Munich Agreement:

At that time – the spring of 1939 – there was no certainty that war was coming. But I wanted to have nothing to do with the military system that, to me, was part of Europe's decay. Mistakenly, as it turned out, I felt that Europe was finished. And it seemed to me that the New World was so much newer, so much readier to welcome new things.[7]

From the deck of the *Ausonia* Britten looked forward to the prospect of concert and commission opportunities, including the intriguing possibility of composing music for a Hollywood film about King Arthur. During the next two and a half years he would try to reconcile a heady intoxication for new things with a yearning for the people, buildings and landscapes left behind.

While visiting Grand Rapids in Michigan shortly after entering the United States from Canada in June 1939, Britten and Pears could not have anticipated that their recently consummated relationship would blossom into a lifelong romantic and musical partnership. Britten's song cycle *Les Illuminations*, begun in Suffolk in March and completed in Long Island in October, included movements dedicated to both Scherchen and Pears. Through the poems of the symbolist poet Arthur Rimbaud, Britten explored the tensions between eroticism and innocence, contrasting the relentless pace and stimuli of urban life with moments of ecstatic serenity. While acknowledging that Rimbaud's texts were enigmatic, Britten was drawn to 'the visions of heaven that were allowed to the poet, and I hope the composer. That is not to say, of course, that the visions are actually of heaven, but rather of the heavenly aspect of the subjects.'[8] Such transporting dreams could offer an escape as Britten anxiously followed developments back in Europe.

Another of the song cycle's dedicatees was Elizabeth Mayer, who along with her husband, Dr William Mayer, became Britten and Pears's most significant supporters and hosts during their time in the United States. The Mayer family had fled Germany piecemeal. In 1933 their daughter, Beata, went to Italy and their son, Michael, to England. Abandoning his medical practice in Munich, William left for the USA in 1936, followed later in the year by Elizabeth and their two remaining children. In 1937 the reunited family made their new home in the village of Amityville, Long Island, forty miles east of Manhattan. They lived in a spacious cottage at the Long Island Home, a psychiatric hospital where William took a job as clinical director, reporting to his younger boss, William Titley.

Elizabeth was a professional translator, a good amateur pianist and a powerful personality, happiest when surrounded by artists, many of whom were also exiles escaping Nazism. Her children soon became accustomed to visits from a circle of friends that included W. H. Auden, Thomas Mann, Albert Einstein, the painter

Josef Scharl and the essayist Giuseppe Antonio Borgese. Elizabeth had first met Pears in 1936 on a ship crossing the Atlantic. In September 1939 she wholeheartedly welcomed Britten and Pears into her home and family.

On 3 September, two days after Hitler invaded Poland and shortly after Bartók had returned from Switzerland to Hungary, Britten wrote his first letter back to England from Amityville. His father had died in 1934, his mother only three years later. Edith Britten had been a good amateur singer whom Benji, as she called him, accompanied on the piano. As Britten adjusted to this loss he found listening to music particularly painful, because it was through music that he had felt most connected to her. During his time in America Britten would find a way to express his grief through his *Sinfonia da Requiem* – a work in fact commissioned by the Japanese government to celebrate the 2,600th anniversary of the Japanese Empire. That the project became a memorial to Britten's parents was a development understandably displeasing to its commissioner.

On New Year's Eve 1939 Britten wrote to his sister Beth from Long Island: 'I'm feeling a bit blue tonight – God how I hate anniversaries – & what with my birthday, Mum's birthday, Xmas & now New Year's Eve – we seem to have a good supply of them recently.'* Britten was grateful to have received cheerful letters from both of his

---

* Britten's mother, Edith Rhoda Britten, had died in 1937. Her birthday was on 9 December.

sisters, even if they had not arrived in time for Christmas. Britten and Pears had spent an enjoyable Christmas with the Mayers:

> In the German custom it was Xmas Eve which was the great hour – at about 6 o'clock a bell was rung & in we all grouped into the living-room & there was an enormous Xmas tree hung all over with candles, candies & cookies & all around the room in little piles were our presents – & lots too – everyone was very generous to us – which made up for lack of correspondence from England![9]

Britten was handsome in a clean-cut, boyish sort of a way, his foppish curly hair, blazer and tie sometimes at odds with a reserved and melancholy demeanour. He was prone to nervous agitation, over-excited by his own artistic pursuits in a strange country where he craved both the intimacy of close relationships and a peaceful working environment. As Britten and Pears settled in at the Long Island Home, this combination of fragility and musical talent was irresistible to Elizabeth Mayer's maternal instincts. In January 1940, when Britten undertook a concert tour in Chicago and Champaign, Illinois, she sounded bereft: 'Everything here awaits you patiently. Your table at the window, the little piece of red blotting paper, which made me cry silently, the ruler . . . the trees and squirrels and the sky. Here is your home now – waiting for you – . . .'[10] Admitting that she had thought of him all day flying like a 'blessed bird' to the Midwest, she complimented her protégé on a quality of 'immortal something' in his music, impatient for his return: 'I long to see you again.' Britten provided both a much-needed link to the world Elizabeth Mayer had left behind and hope for the future. At a time when Britten still grieved the loss of his parents, his host was a stalwart and soothing presence. It was perhaps not a coincidence that Britten described the 'Interlude' movement from *Les Illuminations* dedicated to Mayer as a 'reproof for the exaggeratedly ecstatic mood' of the previous movement, 'Marine'.[11]

In many respects Amityville was an ideal haven for Britten. Although grateful for large audiences, good reviews and unaccustomed publicity, he came quickly to find the dizzying stimuli of New York overwhelming. Both Elizabeth and her daughter Beata assisted Britten by typing letters for him and generally acting as a buffer to the demands of the outside world. After his return from Chicago, Britten was knocked out by a severe streptococcal infection. Beata drew on her expertise as a trained nurse to oversee his recovery, putting in night shifts for a week after his temperature had spiked to 107° and supervising him closely during the next two weeks of prescribed bed rest. Britten would later venture the opinion that Beata had saved his life. During this time Britten jotted down musical ideas in a sketchbook, including a fragment that would become the main theme of the slow movement of his First String Quartet, Opus 25.

Britten was fortunate in finding a congenial living situation but by August 1940 he painted a more complex picture of life in the midst of the psychiatric hospital. Writing to his sister Beth from Maine, he was 'having a much-needed rest from Amityville – the heat and so on'.[12] Tensions had become intolerable between Dr Titley, the director of the Home, and Dr Mayer, who according to Britten was a better doctor than Titley and did not appreciate taking orders from his younger colleague. Despite writing a piano piece for Titley, *Sonata Romantica* – later remembered by Pears as an encouragement to the amateur pianist to practise something other than Weber's *Invitation to a Waltz* – Britten was becoming fed up with the backbiting, lack of privacy and petty scandals. Even Elizabeth Mayer came in for criticism, her lack of tact exposed by the diplomatic balm of Mrs Titley, another doctor at the Home, known in her professional capacity as Mildred Squires. After Britten and Pears left Amityville to visit Maine in the summer of 1940, Elizabeth admitted that it was good for Britten to be elsewhere, especially when she felt unhappy, unbalanced and responsible for a failure of relationships at the Home. Later that summer the Titleys and Mayers were not on speaking terms. In addition to professional tensions, Titley was irritated by Elizabeth's excessive mothering of Britten. Pears did not improve the situation by making off with the young doc-tor's tennis racket.*

While Britten and Pears would remain in contact with the Mayers for many years, the bonds that developed between the travelling musicians and their 'American family', as Elizabeth described it, were not always straightforward to navigate. Britten and Pears relied on the Mayers financially, logistically and for emotional support. For Elizabeth the young men represented the Old World culture she had been forced to leave behind. Close to Britten and yet seemingly blind to his relation-ship with Pears, Elizabeth (according to Michael) even harboured hopes that Britten might marry Beata. In such circumstances a change of scene offered both the possibility of new experiences and an opportunity for disentanglement. Just as Britten had extricated himself from romantic complications in England, now he envi-sioned an escape from the pressure-cooker of the Long Island Home, aware also that Peter's singing career would benefit from him being based in New York for the next season.

For the next six months Britten and Pears experi-mented with a different sort of home environment, sharing a house at 7 Middagh Street in Brooklyn rented by George Davis, an editor at *Harper's Bazaar*, and the

* The Mayers would only stay in Amityville until 1943, William working for much of the rest of his career in New York City at the Hospital for Joint Diseases, and the Neurological Institute.

novelist Carson McCullers. W. H. Auden and American authors Jane and Paul Bowles joined this lively group. Further literary talent was offered in the surprising form of the burlesque entertainer Gypsy Rose Lee, famous not only for her striptease act but also for a best-selling murder mystery written at this time that bore no relationship to a Bach air: *The G-String Murders*. At first Britten and Pears enjoyed the lively company and wild parties that compensated for a general state of disrepair and squalor, but Britten was soon running back to Amityville once a week, declaring it impossible to work in the Brooklyn house. Pears blamed a foot infection on Brooklyn bedbugs, judging that he and Britten were temperamentally unsuited to the chaotic way of life: 'For a short time Middagh Street was kind of fun, but after the tremendous warmth and happiness of Amityville, it wasn't quite home. It was filthy, untidy. Just Bohemia.'[13]

When the pianists Rae Robertson and Ethel Bartlett invited them to California for the summer, Britten and Pears saw a chance once again to escape their current living circumstances. A dry climate seemed preferable to another humid summer on the East Coast, while staying on a ranch in the midst of an orange grove offered the promise of a peaceful working environment unencumbered by personal complications – a good place to work on the new string quartet recently commissioned by Coolidge.

*

Beyond the deck, a robin swooped down in front of me, displacing a rival on the bare flowerbed. *Turdus migratorius.* The name was misleading. While some red-breasted *Turdi* indeed migrated southwards to Texas and Florida during the winter months, many chose to remain, adding fluffier feathers against the cold and adapting their diet from worms to berries. After twenty-seven years of living in Colorado I was still disturbed by this monstrosity with its voluminous gizzard, similar only in colouring to its dainty European namesake.

The restless character of the second movement of Britten's First Quartet had something in common with my mental state. Beyond the deck, my latest lockdown project was a tubular squirrel-proof bird feeder that featured four perches. A solitary red finch had visited several times, on each occasion knocking enough seed to the ground to provide several lurking squirrels with a three-course meal. Under normal circumstances, balancing my teaching and rehearsing at the University of Colorado with concert tours, I would merely have cast the bird feeder an occasional glance, but one evening I had yanked out the pole and pushed it into harder ground between two small trees where I hoped it would attract a greater variety of species. The chickadees remained unimpressed. In front of me the squirrels had taken advantage of my shoddy handiwork to fashion a leaning tower, seed cascading onto the ground below from where they observed me with gluttonous complacency.

Britten's marking of *con slancio* – with enthusiasm and (in this context) momentum – was generated by the driving rhythm of each player playing on every beat. The individual instruments began to assert themselves with impetuous *fortissimo* interjections, often on the second or third beats of the bar, challenging the predictable feeling of three in a bar. These interruptions became more frequent and argumentative until the whole group combined to catapult upwards in a brilliant flourish of triplets. Near the end of the movement the hitherto dependable first beats suddenly disappeared, the enthusiastic driving rhythm that had provided a reassuring frame stuttering to silence. A final emphatic gesture put things to rights but the breakdown of the rhythm seemed to mirror my frequent lockdown progression from frenetic spasms of activity to moments of paralysing self-doubt.

Compared with most people impacted by the virus, I was exceptionally privileged: able to teach my students online, mess around with a bird feeder and sit on my deck listening to a Britten string quartet. But during this period Harumi and I had originally planned a journey to a special place, the sort of pilgrimage of which Britten might have approved. We had booked a flight to Los Angeles, planning to pick up a rental car and drive south along the coast before turning inland to Escondido, twenty miles north of San Diego. I had reserved an Airbnb boasting five-star reviews near the place that Britten and the tenor Peter Pears spent the summer of 1941, hoping to explore

the surrounding area. Instead, using Britten's letters as
a basis, I tried to imagine the unusual conditions under
which he had composed his String Quartet no. 1.

*ARTISTIC RETREAT in Escondido, California,
available from June 1941*
*Your attentive hosts will be renowned pianists Rae Robertson
and Ethel Bartlett, summer renters of this idyllic Sunny
Slopes ranch home from local businessman Ralph Bear. Enjoy
the convivial company of this husband-and-wife piano duo
and excursions to the beach just twenty miles away. On the
ten-acre property you will appreciate relaxing strolls through
the orange grove. A tool shed at the bottom of the garden
provides additional privacy to nurture your most creative
thoughts. This unusual offering would be of particular
interest to fellow musicians.*

REVIEW A June 1941
*A marvellous spot, quiet and high enough above the town
for the temperature to cool down in the evenings. Ideal
conditions for putting the finishing touches to a ballet. For an
Englishman used to the North Sea, hummingbirds and the
occasional coyote add an exotic flavour. The Pacific Ocean is
only twenty miles away and Los Angeles is close enough to
conduct business in Hollywood. For those travelling from the
East Coast, we recommend the experience of driving cross-
country, but it is advisable to service your cooling system
before setting out and practise changing a tyre in case this*

*should become necessary in the desert heat. To prepare for
inspection by the Border Patrol, foreigners should make sure
their visas are current.*

Accommodation 5 stars; Travel 3 stars

REVIEW B July 1941
*Although California offers neither Maine's atmospheric
clifftop walks nor the opportunity to observe seagulls at
any hour of the day, escaping to the ocean for a daily dip
is imperative, given the overbearing tendencies of the hosts.
Shorter visits here are vastly preferable to longer ones. An
unacceptable amount of time and energy may be wasted on
relationships and emotional matters. Musicians beware: four
performers coexisting under one roof is a tinderbox. Although
the sound of the hosts practising piano duos every morning
takes over the whole house, a fan in the tool shed blocks out
much of the racket. Despite everything it is still possible to be
creative here, even to finish a string quartet.*
Location 5 stars; Accommodation 3 stars; Hosts 2 stars

REVIEW C August 1941
*The combination of two pianists practising and the
overpowering heat make it impossible to think straight,
while the sound of planes overhead from a nearby base in
San Diego distracts one with thoughts of war. Spending too
much time in California may inspire disillusion: Hollywood
encourages a sense of unreality, of priorities and values turned
upside-down. Advice for ambitious composers: do not waste*

your energy travelling vast distances in the hope of obtaining film work. Indeed, not to be employed by Hollywood should be considered a lucky escape: composers have no say in the script and gain little or none of the attention and financial rewards showered on the stars. Besides, the musical intelligence of commercial film audiences cannot be underestimated. If you must attend a concert at the Hollywood Bowl, beware: this will not be an authentic musical experience. In addition to incessant discussions of allergies, bowel movements and vitamin supplements, people here drive like maniacs.
Location 3 stars; Hosts 2 stars; Professional Opportunities 0 stars

REVIEW D November 1941
Free rent is an economy that can create an uncomfortable sense of indebtedness: not everyone can toss off a new concerto on Scottish themes to one's hosts as recompense! Two months after the conclusion of our visit it remains no exaggeration to say that the hosts created an intolerable living situation for their guests. One may excuse a degree of selfishness, indulgence and arrogance in the greatest performers but when you combine indifferent talent with unpredictable emotional outbursts, the result is an unpalatable cocktail. Who would have thought that two old gizzards so diminutive in stature would be capable of causing such unpleasantness?! A prison from which you will find yourself relieved to escape.
Overall Rating 1 star

My fictional reviews of Britten's time in Escondido were based only on his letters, just one side of the story. That Britten had changed the nickname of his hosts from 'The Owls' – apparently an affectionate acknowledgement of their short legs – to 'two old gizzards' suggested that something had gone rather wrong during that summer. What had caused the relationships in the orange grove to sour between June and late September 1941? After attending the first performance of his String Quartet on 21 September 1941, given by the Coolidge Quartet at Occidental College outside Los Angeles, Britten returned to New York with Pears, grateful to escape the 'emotional volcano' that he later reported in a letter to his sister Beth. According to the editors of his letters, upsetting scenes 'were caused it seems, by Ethel Robertson (Bartlett) falling hopelessly in love with him during this Californian summer, a situation further complicated by the bizarre position of her husband who was apparently prepared to make a "gift" of his wife to the embarrassed and reluctant composer'.[14] Britten's biographers continue to corroborate this version of events, which is not conclusively proved by the letters themselves. The description of a volcano indeed suggests something more than the usual frictions one might expect between four performing artists living together. Britten was a handsome and talented young man, appealing to both women and men. But the story was an action worthy of at least one contemporary written source. In the absence of any such document, presumably the account was passed on verbally by Britten and Pears to their friends. It is unfortunate that the Robertsons' version of events has not survived.

'From now on maybe you should just play the violin,' our patient landlord suggested as she surveyed the shattered glass from a window frame, shards lodged between the wooden slats of the deck. An over-zealous fling with a weed trimmer had resulted in a rock smashing through the kitchen window. In the absence of concerts, manic home-improvement projects were a warning sign of my temperamental unsuitability to long stretches at home.

Andante calmo, Britten had entitled the third movement of his First Quartet, certainly not a reflection of his living circumstances and most likely composed at a distance from Ethel, Rae and their pianos, in the tool shed at the bottom of the garden. Britten's use of the unusual 5/4 metre created a sense of motion towards the third beat and then a feeling of receding from it, as if one were bobbing up and down in the water. The repetition of the same rhythm in successive bars was in one sense hypnotic but the asymmetric metre was also inherently unstable, as if at any moment the caress of a wave could become unruly. In this way motion and stasis were oddly combined. Listening to the Takács recording of the slow movement, I found our sound to be too direct: perhaps this was a fault of our interpretation, but it also embodied what Britten meant when he questioned the ability of technology to provide a meaningful musical experience. Music that evoked another place was enhanced by being heard at some distance – in a concert-hall acoustic or outside through an open window.

Before I knew anything about the circumstances of the piece's composition, I had described the gloomy North Sea coastline, close to where Britten had purchased the Old Mill in 1937, to an American student quartet who played the piece for me. On the face of it, this was a dubious pedagogical approach, given that Britten had composed the work in the midst of an orange grove, escaping the Robertsons each afternoon to motor down to the beach for a dip in the ocean. Nonetheless, to Elizabeth Mayer Britten reported that although the Pacific was glamorous, he missed the Atlantic. To his sister Beth, Britten wrote that the surfing was better in Cornwall and that he preferred to eat the fish caught in the North Sea, especially a good kipper. Britten had first jotted down fragmentary ideas for this slow movement while recovering from illness in Long Island under the kind supervision of Beata Mayer. Perhaps the *Andante calmo* did after all imagine a faraway seascape, either the Atlantic or the North Sea.

Even in California signs of war encroached on Britten's afternoons at the beach. America had not yet joined the Allies but four months before the bombing of Pearl Harbor, the area north of San Diego was teeming with battleships and aeroplanes. Perhaps the ominous military presence was on Isabel Morse Jones's mind when she reviewed the Coolidge Quartet's premiere of the First Quartet for the *Los Angeles Times*. She particularly praised the *Andante calmo*, assigning it a nostalgic character. 'It might be titled "In Memoriam for a Lost World".'[15] Although I agreed that there was a resigned quality to the first descending first-violin melody, a little later on Britten had employed contrary motion to prepare for my favourite chord of the whole piece: the first violin descended while the cello ascended, the middle voices remaining poised on the same note, all arriving on a chord where the cello G natural and first violin A flat leaned into each other. The mood was ambiguous, this expansive interval of a minor ninth regretful yet full of possibility.

At the end of July Britten concluded his letter to Elizabeth Mayer with a revealing juxtaposition:

> We've just rediscovered the poetry of George Crabbe (all about Suffolk!) & are very excited – maybe an opera one day . . .
> The quartet is in 4 movements (Rondo – Scherzo – Andante – Finale) & in – would you believe it? – D major!![16]

During his Aspen speech in 1964 Britten would later recall that 'coming across a copy of the *Poetical Works* of George Crabbe in a Los Angeles bookshop, I first read

his poem, "Peter Grimes"; and, at the same time reading a most perceptive and revealing article about it by
E. M. Forster I suddenly realised where I belonged and
what I lacked'.[17] Forster's analysis of Crabbe's work and
description of Aldeburgh had pulled at his heartstrings:

> It is a bleak little place: not beautiful. It huddles
> around a flint-towered church and sprawls down to
> the North Sea – and what a wallop the sea makes as it
> pounds at the shingle! Nearby is a quay, at the side of
> an estuary, and here the scenery becomes melancholy
> and flat; expanses of mud, saltish commons, the marsh-
> birds crying. Crabbe heard that sound and saw that
> melancholy, and they got into his verse.[18]

That Crabbe never escaped the spirit of Aldeburgh was
in Forster's opinion essential to his artistic voice. Forster
went on to link the melancholy scenery with the troubled character of the protagonist in Crabbe's grim story
of the ostracised fisherman, Peter Grimes, suspected of
murdering his apprentices. He ended the article by urging his readers to read the biography written by Crabbe's
son and discover 'how the poor little boy who rolled
barrels on the quay at Aldeburgh made good'. Forster's
essay triggered both Britten's nostalgia and visions for
the future. Perhaps Aldeburgh could infuse his music as
much as it had Crabbe's poetry.

*

Whether in *Les Illuminations* or in the slow music of his First String Quartet, some of Britten's most evocative music took the form of interludes: suspended moments of uneasy calm between past and future events. Given the purported emotional volcano that Britten had experienced in Escondido, it is fair to assume that the slow movement of the quartet did not rejoice in the present. Nevertheless its effect on me during the sixth week of stay-at-home was to make me reconsider the idea of interludes. In order for music to take one to a different time and place, there was some advantage to being suspended, to not going anywhere oneself. Unable to travel, I felt wistful as I relived Britten's yearning for Aldeburgh and his decision to return to England. His subsequent decision to put down roots as he embraced his new life in Suffolk was however a useful antidote to the ingrained restlessness so typical of the travelling musician. I turned off the stereo system, filled a carton with sunflower seed, walked across the deck and repositioned the feeder on its original spot. The chickadees were back, their calls as persistent as ever. For the first time since lockdown I felt like giving Boulder at least a four-star review.

On 7 June 1945, one month after VE Day and three years after Britten and Pears returned to England, Britten's opera *Peter Grimes* received its premiere at the Sadler's Wells Theatre in London. Pears sang the title role. The sense of uneasy calm and undulating melodic lines in the slow movement of the First Quartet surfaced again in one of the opera's orchestral interludes. 'Moonlight' was later published as a part of a separate orchestral piece, *Four Sea Interludes from 'Peter Grimes'*.

In the summer of 1947 Britten and Pears moved from Snape to Crabbe Street in Aldeburgh. For the next decade they made the three-storey Crag House their home, Britten's first-floor study providing a sea view. Almost immediately they began to explore the musical possibilities within the Aldeburgh community. Along with Eric Crozier, the first director of *Peter Grimes*, Britten and Pears announced the first annual Festival of Music and Painting, to take place in Aldeburgh in June 1948. Britten's opera *Albert Herring* was performed at the Jubilee Hall, a few steps down Crabbe Street from Crag House. E. M. Forster gave a lecture at this first festival, staying in Crag House where his hosts played and sang for him. Britten's enthusiasm for music-making at his home found a further outlet in 1952, when he and Pears formed the Aldeburgh Music Club. Membership was restricted to thirty-five local players and singers, amateur or professional, who were invited to join by a committee. Rehearsals took place in Crag House. The members of the Club participated in Festival events including innovative open-air concerts that took place on the Thorpeness Meare boating lake. Britten and Pears played in the recorder ensemble, under the watchful eye of conductor Imogen Holst.

With this extraordinary venue in mind, Britten composed his *Six Metamorphoses after Ovid*, Opus 49, for solo
oboe, first performed at the 1951 Aldeburgh Festival by
its dedicatee, Joy Cooper. Unencumbered by underlying harmonies, the solo musical line – the same music
that my gran would later practise in her Shropshire cottage – floated across the water. During the fifth piece,
'Narcissus' ('who fell in love with his own image and
became a flower'), the oboist could even glance down into
the water and catch her own reflection in the Meare.

Throughout his life Britten was a prolific correspondent. On 19 January 1930, aged sixteen, he had written to
his parents from his boarding school, Gresham's, imagining his letter being transported by the Midland and
Great Northern Railway and deposited on their doorstep
at around quarter to eight on a Monday morning. He

envied his parents for the warmth of their fire at home: in his new miserable living situation the water pipes were colder than his hands. He asked them to send his love to his sister Beth, brother Bobby, Aunt Queenie and Seizer, the family's springer spaniel. Six years later, trains were again on his mind when he composed the music for *Night Mail*. Auden's poem imagines the inhabitants of Glasgow, Edinburgh and Aberdeen awakening, their hearts quickening as they hear the postman knocking, hoping that they will not be forgotten. During his American sojourn, Britten's frequent letters home to England to his sisters and friends expressed not only nostalgia but a fervent desire to keep ties alive until friendships could be resumed in familiar landscapes. By writing letters home, Britten countered his own fear of being forgotten.

After moving to Aldeburgh in 1947, only twenty-eight miles south of Lowestoft where he had spent the first fifteen years of his life, Britten not only reconnected with his childhood but also inspired a rich musical life on his doorstep. As he later explained during his Aspen speech: 'I write music, now, in Aldeburgh, for people living there, and further afield, indeed for anyone who cares to play it or listen to it. But my music now has its roots, in where I live and work. And I only came to realise that in California in 1941.'[19]

A Chorus of Birds

Above the Port Williams beach, trees jut out from the bluff, 'hanging on for dear life', as Richard describes them. When he returns to his hometown of Sequim, northwest of Seattle, he walks along the westerly promontory where many years ago he scattered his grandmother's ashes. Growing up with his mother Bok-Soon Lee and her American adoptive parents, Richard listened to his grandparents' *Reader's Digest* boxed sets of LPs in the living room of their mobile home, set on five acres of land outside town. Later his grandfather bought him his first boom box. Music was a refuge: racist taunts on the school bus and jokes about his developmentally disabled mother exacerbated Richard's sense of being an outsider. He was grateful to find musical mentors who ran the local youth orchestra nearby, and to encounter string quartets at the nearby Olympic Music Festival, founded by Alan Iglitzin, violist of the Philadelphia String Quartet.

Las Vegas, Nevada. Winston-Salem, North Carolina. Los Angeles. New York. After Richard left Sequim at the age of fifteen to pursue his education, music and travel became entwined. As a graduate student at the Juilliard School, he began to perform frequently in Korea, sometimes making five or six trips there each year. He became accustomed to the idea of home as the place at times 'where you just happen to rest your head'.

Now in his early forties, while he juggled worldwide travel and appearances as a soloist and chamber musician, Richard felt at something of a crossroads. He was attracted to the idea of digging deeply into quartet repertoire, our residency at the University of Colorado and regular rehearsal schedule. Upon his return from Korea in May 2020, he quarantined, packed up his car and began to drive east. I would not have relished the experience of driving at night over the Continental Divide but Richard stopped to sleep on a mattress in the back of his car and enjoyed approaching the Front Range west of Boulder as the sun lit up the Flatirons. His move to Boulder would offer the chance to adjust the balance between home and life on the road – if not precisely in the way COVID-19 had so far dictated.

From a nearby store, No Place Like Home, I decide to purchase an assortment of rehearsal chairs of varied heights and padding. As the virus spreads it seems safest to convert our living room into a rehearsal space, the high wooden ceilings contributing to a favourable acoustic. András brings his own lower chair and a pine board shaped like a large fish that he had many years ago fashioned with a jig saw, using a drill press to make holes for the chair's front legs and a handle. Riddled with indentations from his cello spike, the board not only protects carpets but acts as a sounding board, particularly on stages lacking wooden floors. Whereas Harumi's early Takács Quartet experiences took place on the road, with Richard we spend almost all our time together at home preparing for video projects. Sometimes we crowd around a computer screen on our sofa to record greetings for our audiences or participate in live post-concert discussions. Our only livestreamed concerts take place at the University of Colorado in the empty Grusin Music Hall.

During the first week of January 2021, in preparation for one such concert, we begin to rehearse Britten's String Quartet no. 3, Opus 94. Britten completed the work in November 1975, the same month in which he celebrated his sixty-second birthday. The first movement of this five-movement piece, composed for the Amadeus Quartet and dedicated to Austrian-emigré musicologist Hans Keller, is entitled 'Duets' and features all the different combinations of instruments playing in pairs. 'Duets' is in some ways an ideal exercise for a group working with a new member, allowing each pair of players to match rhythms, sounds and phrase shapes. Harumi and Richard are responsible for setting the opening mood; the first eleven bars are for second violin and viola alone. Close in pitch to each other, they take turns to play the primary melodic line. Syncopation between the two parts in a *piano* dynamic creates a sense of undulation. How clearly one articulates the rhythm influences the character. In the Amadeus Quartet's recording of the piece for Deutsche

Grammophon, second violinist Siegmund Nissel and violist Peter Schidlof adopt a muscular approach, playing with an intensity that immediately conveys a sense of foreboding. Given their close association with Britten, the Amadeus's interpretation is the starting point for any group but I prefer the application of less defined and breathier bow-strokes to create a more mysterious mood. The idea has its pitfalls. Later in the opening section, András and I play a similar duet. There is too much mystery in our rhythm, caused by indistinct bow changes and my bad habit of hanging on to tied notes for too long. We have been playing together for so long that we make instinctive adjustments to each other, but our unpredictable course is unnerving to our fellow travellers. As we try to play our rhythm with more precision, we discover a natural ebb and flow within each bar. András suggests that the oscillating quavers between the two instruments represent a gondolier propelling his boat forward. At the end of the bar the smoother rhythm and melodic contour suggest less momentum as he lifts his oar. Richard points out further benefits to a less angular feeling in the opening section of the movement. This approach sets up more contrast with his later duet with András where they throw abrupt chords back and forth, stubbornness replacing fluidity. But in this duet they worry that the music has become too choppy and vertical: they experiment with moving through the semiquavers that precede each group of chords, adding an element of anxiety. As we continue to balance the different elements in 'Duets', Harumi draws attention to the music's ambiguous character. To experience the lilting motion of the ocean may be hypnotic, but the latent power of the undercurrent is simultaneously unsettling, reminding us of forces beyond our control.

If in some ways this introspective music does not match the mood of expectancy that accompanies the addition of a new player, in other respects it is a perfect work to play during a pandemic. In May 1973 Britten had undergone heart surgery to replace a valve. During the six-hour operation he suffered a small stroke that compromised his right-hand co-ordination, especially upsetting to an accomplished pianist accustomed to trying out his new compositions at the keyboard. Britten's fragile health provided the backdrop for this Third Quartet, in which he revisited his earlier opera *Death in Venice*, based on Thomas Mann's novella, quoting several themes from the opera at the beginning of the quartet's last movement. Aschenbach, a writer struggling to rekindle his creativity, returns to Venice. He is inspired by the young boy Tadzio but his obsession with Tadzio's beauty leads him to remain too long in Venice, where he succumbs to the cholera epidemic spreading through the city.

Britten composed most of the quartet in Aldeburgh in October 1975. In November Bill Servaes (general manager of the Aldeburgh Festival) and his wife Patricia took Britten and his nurse Rita Thomson back to Venice, where they stayed at the Hotel Danieli. Here Britten continued work on the final movement of the quartet, 'La Serenissima'. Thomson described how the party explored Venice in the mornings, taking *vaporetti* all over the city to view pictures, carrying Britten over bridges in his wheelchair. In the afternoon Thomson 'would get Ben up at about 4 o'clock, and go out for a walk, leaving him by the window, listening to the bells. I used to open the window, and you know how in Venice you hear one bell, and then another, and then a few more – he adored that.'[1]

The opening section of 'La Serenissima' culminates with the same musical theme that Aschenbach uses in the opera to declare to Tadzio, 'I love you!' Harumi and Richard are left holding a C pedal note and a passacaglia begins.[2] András repeats an insistent bass line beneath a melody that I play first, followed at twelve-bar intervals by Harumi and Richard. When András takes over the melody, Richard assumes the bass line. We find it hard to gauge the dramatic balance between melody and unyielding bass. Britten marks each entrance of the melody at a higher dynamic, but as our volume increases we are tripping along, the melody too easily sloughing off its burden. Even the ecstatic cascades of bells that occur roughly two-thirds of the way through the movement should be pinned back by András's notes, under which Britten has written 'very marked'.

On 8 December 1975 the young composer Colin Matthews returned to Aldeburgh for a second session of work on the quartet with Britten. To help Britten realise his intentions, Matthews played the piece through on the piano, making changes to the score as Britten reacted to hearing his quartet for the first time. Britten joined in for the passacaglia, playing the cello part on the piano with his still-strong left hand. With this in mind we try the opening again, this time not allowing the melody quite the same degree of independence from a recurring bass line that is the most significant feature of the movement.

In September 1976 the members of the Amadeus Quartet travelled to Aldeburgh to play the new quartet for the ailing Britten in The Red House, a large farm-house situated next to a golf course half a mile inland from Crabbe Street. Britten and Pears had moved there in 1957, giving up their sea view to swap houses with their friend, the artist Mary Potter. Their fame had made Crag House an impractical residence, passers-by peering over the fence or through the holes after a taller fence was erected. Britten supervised the conversion of one of the outhouse buildings at The Red House into a music studio, where he could compose and play the piano without fear of disturbing anyone. To the main building Britten and Pears added a library – it was here that the Amadeus Quartet played for the composer. Peter Schidlof recalled that although Britten could only manage to work with them for roughly twenty minutes at a time, he was as exacting as ever, instructing the players on the ebb and flow of the music while at the same time assuring them that he trusted their judgement. Unconfident of the piece's merit, Britten was reassured after hearing the Amadeus's private performance. For Schidlof and his colleagues, the excitement of participating in the genesis of this new work was tempered by unease as they observed Britten's increased frailty.

Britten composed the piece with the Amadeus in mind, no more so than the third movement, entitled 'Solo', in which he conceived an extraordinary first violin part for Norbert Brainin. A bird soars unencumbered, later joined by a chorus of birds in an ecstatic middle section. To evoke the chorus the first violin jumps fiendishly across strings while the second violin plays fast *pizzicati*, the viola fast arpeggios and the cello *glissandi* high up the fingerboard. This disembodied quality is intensified in the last section. While the first violin continues the high melody, the other three parts climb higher and higher up their respective lower strings, not fully stopping the notes to create the natural harmonic series, left hands almost touching bows as the music resolves to a C major chord. The first violin descends, leaving the others in the stratosphere, all its notes within the same chord, coming to rest on a middle C. For the last few bars, Britten had composed several alternatives for this descending line, worried that this last extended C major tonality was too straightforwardly diatonic, but decided not to change it.[3] At the very top of the fingerboard the notes are extremely close together, a millimetre the difference between consonance and a rudely dissonant note. As the first violin descends, the fragility of the consonant chord prevents it from ever sounding bland.

Britten composed most of the quartet at The Red House and worked on the last movement in Venice. 'Solo' was inspired by a third location. In 1970, to escape the stresses associated with running the Aldeburgh Festival and the sound of the low-flying planes from a nearby American base, Britten and Pears had purchased a cottage outside Horham, a village twenty-five miles inland from Aldeburgh. At the bottom of the garden Britten had a small hut built as a composition studio, looking out over an empty field. Even in Horham planes sometimes still disturbed the composer, but it was here that he worked on 'Solo', its middle section inspired by intoxicating birdsong. Britten had moved from Crag House to The Red House to avoid prying eyes; from there he retreated to Horham. But whether on a beach in California or in a studio at the bottom of a garden in Suffolk, tranquillity was elusive. Paradoxically, home included the idea of an escape, a retreat to elsewhere.

We miss the sounds of enthusiastic chatter in the hall as we tune our instruments backstage before our live-streamed concert in Grusin Music Hall. When we walk on stage, our feet clatter over the resonant wooden floor. András supervised its refurbishment a decade ago, ensuring a hollow resonating chamber beneath his cello spike, a more elegant solution than his wooden fish. I try to imagine our friends listening over loudspeakers in their living rooms and my parents who will watch our performance the next day in Cambridge, in the same room next to the kitchen where I used to practise over forty years ago. To suppress a cough brought on by the dry climate, I slip a menthol drop into my mouth underneath my mask. Now it adds an extra sting to the hot breath that fogs my glasses. The facial clues that we usually rely on to communicate changes of character are hidden behind our masks. From the glint in Richard's right eye I can imagine his smile. András's eyebrows, sometimes raised sceptically against the dubious musical ideas of a first violinist, now seem manically animated.

Before we begin to play 'Solo', I recall Norbert Brainin's last letter to Britten, written on 30 November 1976:

> I am so sorry to hear that you are not well. Please not to worry about the quartet. We are practising and we remember everything you told us. The boys send you their love. We hope you will be well enough to come to the concert on Dec. 19. Please get well soon.[4]

Britten would not be in the hall for the concert: he died on December 4.

Britten explained to Colin Matthews that he intended the quartet to end with a question. At the bottom of the last chord, the same D natural that throughout the movement has questioned the E major tonality clashes with a C sharp, E and G sharp in the three other parts. Britten's *rinforzando* encourages us to emphasise the dissonance before receding. The D natural is left hanging on after the other notes have ended, refusing to resolve. During our stage rehearsal before the concert András wonders if our attack on the chord has become too angry and explicit, considering the weary tread of the previous music. Richard suggests reversing the bowing to end on an up-bow; in the lightest part of the bow we can lean into the note without the risk of an abrasive beginning to the note. But that is less practical for András, who has to hold his note for longer: he will end up trying to fade out as he approaches the frog, the heaviest part of the bow. In the concert we try Richard's unusual solution: the three of us retain the up-bow but András ends on a down-bow. This lack of unanimity emphasises the independence of the D natural and gives a visual dimension to the lack of resolution.

Compared with the torturous anguish that dominates *Death in Venice*, the passacaglia that ends this quartet is more serene. In my introductory words to our online audience I suggest that Britten's music can offer consolation, connecting us over distance. As we approach the last phrase of the piece in the empty Grusin Music Hall, I am not so sure. The silence after András's note fades away may be more effective when not followed by a tentative trickle of applause, but Britten was right to acknowledge the limitations of loudspeakers: it is only an act of communion between live audience and performers that reveals the many dimensions of this bleak yet comforting music.

Towards the end of Kenneth Grahame's *The Wind in the Willows* the devious and narcissistic Toad returns home to Toad Hall.[5] As part of a celebratory banquet he devises a concert with a unified theme. A Speech by Toad will be followed by an Address by Toad, a Song by Toad, more Speeches by Toad throughout the evening and other compositions by Toad – sung by the composer himself. But Toad's long-suffering friends Badger, Rat and Mole forbid such a shameless show of vanity, urging Toad to use his homecoming as an opportunity to turn over a new leaf. Cowed into submission the thwarted impresario retreats to his bedroom to ponder his predicament:

> At last he got up, locked the door, drew the curtains across the windows, collected all the chairs in the room and arranged them in a semicircle, and took up his position in front of them, swelling visibly. Then he bowed, coughed twice, and, letting himself go, with uplifted voice he sang, to the enraptured audience that his imagination so clearly saw.[6]

Toad finds the experience cathartic. During the banquet he is a changed character, so modest and well behaved that some of the guests wonder if the party is perhaps not quite as fun as those thrown previously at Toad Hall.

Inside the front cover of my hardback copy of the book is an inscription from my Mondaytown grandparents. I had remembered nothing about Toad's concert, only his antics and misdemeanours, delightfully outrageous to a six-year-old. Now I find it hard to believe in his character transformation, a narcissist addicted to performance and applause miraculously humbled by the censure of his friends. Banished to his bedroom nowadays, there would be no need for Toad to gather chairs for an imaginary audience, YouTube Live one of many available platforms with which to reach a real audience – during a pandemic he might even have time to write a book. Within most musicians lies an element of Toad, a craving for performances, audiences and recognition. My plan had been to end my book, if not triumphantly, at least in a celebratory mood as the Takács Quartet returned to the stage in Budapest, London, Tokyo or at Richard's own festival in Sequim. Toad's concert has taken the lustre off the idea.

During a rehearsal break we sit around the kitchen table spreading Harumi's feta, dill and yoghurt dip over matzah. Until recently I had been ignorant of matzah's central role in Seder, the feast that begins Passover: it symbolises the unleavened bread the Jews carried on their backs after being forced to flee Egypt. Our crispy gluten-free variety and recreational eating is far removed from matzah's traumatic origins. András has contributed traditional Hungarian meatballs (*fasirt*) prepared by his wife Kati, smoked paprika its crucial ingredient. For dessert Richard brings local baker Johnny Sugar's Pecan Coffee chocolates. With rehearsal snacks as good as these there is little incentive to leave the table.

For each of us music and food have been closely connected since childhood. During my early-morning practice sessions in Cambridge I could hear my father preparing breakfast in the adjoining kitchen, sometimes opening the small hatch between rooms to hand me a sweetened cup of tea and a piece of toast liberally spread with butter and strawberry jam. After concerts my mother hosted small parties at home, facilitating a festive atmosphere. Whatever mishaps had occurred on stage, I came away with a positive memory of the whole concert experience.

From an early age András associated chamber music with dessert. At weekends his father, a professional cellist and conductor, invited friends and colleagues over to the family's apartment in Budapest to play quartets, quintets and sextets. At first, András and his younger brother György, a violinist, merely listened and devoured their mother's floating island desserts. Later they were allowed to join in the music-making. As a counterbalance to such rarefied experiences, when their parents were out György instigated scientific experiments with their mother's hairspray, lighting cans in the corridor to create impressive flame-throwers.

Harumi also grew up in a family of chamber musicians: her father Samuel Rhodes was violist of the Juilliard Quartet for forty-seven years; her mother Hiroko Yajima was second violinist in the Galimir Quartet and later a member of the Mannes Trio. Harumi began playing the violin at the age of seven, at first practising in the kitchen between the stove and the kitchen table. Hiroko would never formally have offered practice bribes, but as Harumi came to the end of an assignment, the readiness of the curly pasta swirls in tomato sauce would sometimes happen to require testing.

In Sequim, growing one's own produce was a way of life. During the summer months Richard pulled up weeds; as he grew older he helped aerate the soil with his grandparents' rototiller. Of the various vegetables and fruits his grandparents harvested, Richard's favourite were the gooseberries that his grandmother baked into pies, a delectable complement to his exploration of Wagner and Strauss over loudspeakers. When Richard goes back to Sequim now, a fresh Dungeness crab, shucked and shelled, is his favourite pre- or post-concert delicacy.

In our new formation *gulyás* and chips is no longer a suitable Takács meal. Harumi suggests that in our hotpot we could combine Hungarian meatballs with Korean and Japanese staples. As yet, for some reason, no one has lobbied to add an English element to this mix. From the online store Home Basket, I think I have found a solution. I place a large bottle of Worcestershire sauce on the table, arguably an even more successful English export than Elgar's music.

'It's perfect for us: organic ingredients gathered from all over the world, kosher, kind of like soy sauce but less salty. You can dip meatballs in it – Japanese cookbooks even include it as a special ingredient.'

'I'm surprised you like it. I thought you hated vinegar,' Harumi says. 'And you can get soy sauce with less sodium – that comes in the bottle with the green lid.'

'Woo-se-che-ster,' András tries out the syllables. 'Is that right?'

'Good enough,' I say, encouraged by András's interest.

'My grandfather used to pour it all over his meat. "Like soy sauce": isn't that a stretch?' Richard screws up his mouth in an amused if mildly disgusted grimace.

András studies the Lea & Perrins label, boasting unmatchable flavour since 1835. 'Is there a French version I could stick to?'

'You might stand a better chance if you cooked with it instead of just putting it on the table,' says Harumi.

My introduction of Worcestershire sauce seems to have ended the rehearsal break: the others stand up and walk back to our living room. Harumi's suggestion is pragmatic: after years of experience discussing and trying out musical ideas, I should know that a theoretical argument is less persuasive than its practical application. Given the propensity of quartet players to change opinions from one rehearsal to the next, perhaps this fermented condiment might become as popular as Harumi's feta and dill dip, its rejection not necessarily a fetaccompli.

Beneath the camaraderie of extended rehearsal breaks and my unnecessary puns lies an undercurrent of anxiety. For the Takács, will the pandemic prove to be an interlude banished by a reassuring return to normality? Even when concerts resume, I wonder if I will suffer a loss of nerve either in my own playing or in the sustainability of an enterprise that can be so comprehensively swept aside by a virus. What would be a suitable collective noun to describe our quartet in these circumstances? Certainly not a pride of lions. We are more like a chorus of birds: our daily routines provide structure but the sounds that we create are ephemeral, vanishing into the air. We are a trembling of finches.

Today we are working on Haydn's last unfinished string quartet, Opus 103. Haydn planned his Opus 77 quartets to be part of a six-quartet set, but those two pieces and the middle two movements of this third quartet (published separately and assigned a different opus number) were all that he managed to complete. At the bottom of the score he added a quote from his chorale 'Der Greis', with the words underneath, 'Gone is all my strength, old and weak am I.'

Both the movements have an ABA structure. Ever since I first encountered Haydn quartets as a teenager at Chesterton School, I have generally been less engaged by this symmetrical form, preferring the demonic transformations to which Bartók subjects his A sections, but these two Haydn movements are swaying my opinion. As the first movement unfolds, surprising harmonic shifts and dynamic contrasts challenge the contented character of the opening melody. Towards the end Haydn adds a coda that features a hesitant fragment of this same tune, the cello at first dropping out and then joining in with a mysterious bass note that briefly undermines the group. Richard suggests that we pause before this coda, allowing the section to stand separately from what has come before, emphasising its fractured nature. The abruptness with which the cello banishes this moment of doubt by pulling us back to the home key is oddly forced, the final cadence emphatic yet unconvincing.

Doubt returns in the main section of the second movement, a minuet in D minor. Harumi asks if we could try playing the opening less politely, with more sense of danger and storminess – the protestations of someone who has been wronged. In the second section of the Minuet the first violin and cello introduce a rising chromatic figure, dissonant notes clashing against unchanging notes in the inner voices. After an ominous pause the idea is extended, the first violin climbing up the E string, directionless, unhinged, before a dramatic scale and cadence return us to the home key. András is keen that we should not play this chromatic creeping with any sense of flow – it should sound as though we have lost our way. Following a radiant, lilting trio, the return of the Minuet is all the more devastating, its eerie chromatic lines and inner agitation a poignant and incomplete statement by the most prolific composer of the genre.

A string quartet's work is always unfinished, familiar pieces revealing new facets, particularly in the presence of new players. Our choice not to rush through this music comes only partly from a desire to bring out Haydn's astounding originality. The pain and struggle that lie behind Haydn's last unfinished quartet cast the minuet form in a different light. In our makeshift quartet home where we rehearse and wonder what the future will bring, we are drawn to those moments of disorientation, the way in which Haydn enables a sense of being anchored and an equally strong sense of being cast off to coexist uneasily within the same frame. I am growing to like minuets, the capacity that this music has to take us both home and beyond.

Acknowledgements

When I wrote about my dear friend Roger Tapping's approach to page turns in Bartók's First Quartet, I did not know that as I was approaching the end of the copyediting process for *Distant Melodies*, he would die from cancer. Between 1995 and 2005 we shared a musical home: I was very fortunate that he was the Takacs's violist during that decade and remain so grateful for his musicianship, steadying influence, mischievous sense of humour and generous attitude to playing chamber music. Roger loved Elgar's Piano Quintet and provided helpful feedback on the first sections of my book.

Throughout the evolution of this project I have been indebted to David Lawrence Morse for his painstaking reading and astute comments. Thanks to Martin Dusinberre for sharing his vivid childhood memories of Mondaytown. Many thanks to my other readers – Christopher Adey, Richard Beales, Steven Bruns, Daniel Chua, Seldy Cramer, Tim Dawkins, John Kongsgaard, Nick Mathew and Michael Turelli – all of whose contributions greatly improved the book. I am so grateful to Belinda Matthews at Faber for believing in the project and helping to shape it, and to Michael Downes and Joanna Harwood for their expertise and good humour in the later production stages. Colin Matthews offered crucial insight and details for my Britten chapters. Thanks to Nick Clark at the Britten-Pears Archive in Aldeburgh, John Burkhalter for helping me access Elgar's diaries in Princeton, Aspen Hill at the Escondido Public Library, David Beveridge, Terry Heard from the Dvořák Society and Sharon Lu at HKU. I owe much to my agent Rebecca Carter at Janklow and Nesbit, for her guidance and encouragement, and for her necessary input many years ago as the violist in our Chesterton School String Quartet.

This book is of course only possible because of my colleagues in the Takács Quartet. Learning more about Harumi, Richard and András's backgrounds, upbringing and different ideas of home has been one of the joys of this project. In addition to reading many versions of the different chapters, Harumi has contributed thought-provoking insights about both the music and our lives together. This book has been greatly enriched by her perspective.

I am grateful to the *Massachusetts Review* for granting me permission to use a section about Bartók's Sixth Quartet that appeared in a different form on 11 October 2019 as an article entitled 'At a Distance: Sadness in Bartók's Final Quartet'.

List of Permissions

Picture Credits

39. Elgar's Map, 1921. Royal College of Music Collections, Object Number PPHC000176 Royal College of Music/ ArenaPAL.

91. Dvořák with his pigeons. Inventory number č. S 226/1072. Permission is given by National Museum – Czech Museum of Music, Prague, Czech Republic.

105. Annotated Bartók score. Courtesy of the author.

126. Bartók in Anatolia, 1936, kindly provided by the Bartók Archives of the Institute for Musicology, Research Centre for the Humanities.

190. Benjamin Britten and Peter Pears with Aldeburgh Music Club on Thorpeness Meare, Suffolk © Marion Thorpe, 17 June 1954. Image provided by Britten Pears Arts (brittenpearsarts.org). Ref: PH/5/119.

210. Photo of Takács Quartet, Boulder, 21 June 2020 © Amanda Tipton.

Text Permissions

Excerpt from Tom Stoppard, *The Invention of Love* (London, Faber, 1997). *The Invention of Love* © 1997 by Tom Stoppard. Used by permission of United Agents LLP. Reproduced with permission from Faber and Faber Ltd.

Excerpt from *Nocturnes: Five Stories of Music and Nightfall* by Kazuo Ishiguro. Published by Faber & Faber. Copyright © Kazuo Ishiguro. Reproduced by permission of the author c/o Rogers, Coleridge & White Ltd., 20 Powis Mews, London W11 1JN. Copyright © 2009 Kazuo Ishiguro and reproduced with permission from Vintage Canada/Alfred A. Knopf Canada, a division of Penguin Random House Canada Limited. All rights reserved.

Antonín Dvořák, *Letters and Reminiscences*, Otakar Šourek (ed.), trans. Roberta Finlayson Samsour, 1954.

Willa Cather, *My Antonia*, 1918.

W. H. Reed, *Elgar as I Knew Him*, 1936.

Béla Bartók: Letters by Béla Bartók, collected, selected, edited and annotated by János Demény, trans. Péter Balabán and István Farkas, trans. revised by Elisabeth West and Colin Mason (Budapest, 1971). Reproduced with permission from Faber and Faber Ltd.

Works Cited

Allis, Michael. 'Elgar, Lytton and the Piano Quintet, Op. 84', in *Music & Letters*, vol. 85, no. 2. Oxford, 2004.

Barr, Cyrilla. *Elizabeth Sprague Coolidge: American Patron of Music.* New York, 1998.

Bartók, Béla. *Essays.* Benjamin Suchoff (ed.). London, 1976.

—— *Letters.* Collected, selected, edited and annotated by János Demény, translated by Péter Balabán and István Farkas; translation revised by Elisabeth West and Colin Mason. Budapest, 1971.

Beckerman, Michael. *New Worlds of Dvořák.* New York, 2003.

Beveridge, David. 'Dvořák's Abodes and Travels During the First Years of His Marriage (1873–77)', in Graham Melville-Mason (ed.), *Czech Music*, vol. 25. Bramley, 2014.

Britten, Benjamin. *Letters from a Life: The Selected Letters and Diaries of Benjamin Britten.* Donald Mitchell, Philip Reed and Mervyn Cooke (eds). 6 vols. London, 1991.

—— *On Receiving the First Aspen Award.* London, 1964.

Cather, Willa. *My Antonia.* Boston, 1918.

Dusinberre, Juliet. *Alice to the Lighthouse: Children's Books and Radical Experiments in Art*. London, 1987.

Dusinberre, William. *Them Dark Days*. Oxford, 1996.

Dvořák, Antonín. *Letters and Reminiscences*. Otakar Šourek (ed.), trans. Roberta Finlayson Samsour. Prague, 1954.

Dvořák, Otakar. *Antonín Dvořák, My Father*. Paul J. Polansky (ed.), trans. Miroslav Němec. Spillville, IA, 1993.

Elgar, Edward. *Letters of a Lifetime*. Jerrold Northrop Moore (ed.). London, 2012.

Floyd, Ted. 'Reassessment of a Scarlet Tanager from Spillville, Iowa: Was It Really a Tanager?', in *Iowa Bird Life*, vol. 86, no. 4. Johnston, IA, 2016.

Grahame, Kenneth. *The Wind in the Willows*. Oxford, 1908.

Immerwahr, Daniel. *How to Hide an Empire*. New York, 2019.

Ishiguro, Kazuo. *Nocturnes*. London, 2009.

Ivanov, Miraslav. *In Dvořák's Footsteps: Musical Journeys in the New World*. Leon Karel (ed.), trans. Stania Slahor. Kirksville, MO, 1995.

Kildea, Paul. *Benjamin Britten: A Life in the Twentieth Century*. London, 2013.

Leafstedt, Carl. 'Asheville, Winter of 1943–44: Bela Bartók and North Carolina', in *Musical Quarterly*, vol. 87, no. 2. Oxford, 2004.

Matthews, Colin. 'Working Notes', in Alan Blyth, *Remembering Britten*. London, 1981.

P. Ovidius Naso. *Metamorphoses*. Trans. Arthur Golding. Boston, 1922. Perseus Digital Library. http://www. perseus.tufts.edu.

Reed, W. H. *Elgar as I Knew Him*. Oxford, New York, 1989.

Riley, Matthew. *Elgar and the Nostalgic Imagination*. Cambridge, 2007.

Shafak, Elif. 'Exile', in Sigrid Rausing (ed.), *Granta* no. 149. London, 2019.

Stoppard, Tom. *The Invention of Love*. London, 1997.

Tibbetts, John C. (ed.). *Dvořák in America, 1892–1895*. Portland, OR, 1993.

Tyrrell, John. 'Forster, Crabbe and Britten, *The Listener*, 29 May 1941'. https://john-tyrrell.blogspot. com/2014/09/forster-crabbe-and-britten.html, last accessed 16 December 2020.

Notes

HERE AND ELSEWHERE
1 Elif Shafak, 'Exile', in Sigrid Rausing (ed.), *Granta* no. 149 (London, 2019), pp. 234–5.
2 Tom Stoppard, *The Invention of Love* (London, 1997), p. 29.
3 *The Times*, 24 February 1934.

ELGAR'S HILLS
1 https://laserops.co.uk, last accessed 14 December 2020.
2 Kazuo Ishiguro, *Nocturnes* (London, 2009), p. 94.
3 *Nocturnes*, p. 121.

ELGAR'S RETREAT: WHAT REMAINS
1 W. H. Reed, *Elgar as I Knew Him* (Oxford, New York, 1989), pp. 56–7.
2 Reed, p. 58.
3 Reed, p. 59.
4 Reed, p. 60.
5 Reed, p. 63.
6 See Michael Allis, 'Elgar, Lytton and the Piano Quintet, Op. 84', *Music & Letters*, vol. 85, no. 2 (Oxford, 2004), pp. 198–238.
7 Reed, p. 69.
8 Matthew Riley, *Elgar and the Nostalgic Imagination* (Cambridge, 2007), p. 37.
9 https://shropshire.gov.uk/committee-services/documents/ s20182/Item%207%20-%201%20Monday%20Town%20-%2018- 02962-FUL.pdf, last accessed 18 February 2021.

FREEDOM'S SOIL: DVOŘÁK AT HOME AND ABROAD
1 Ted Floyd, 'Reassessment of a Scarlet Tanager from Spillville, Iowa: Was It Really a Tanager?', *Iowa Bird Life*, vol. 86, no. 4 (Johnston, IA, 2016), pp. 159–61.
2 Antonín Dvořák, *Letters and Reminiscences*, Otakar Šourek (ed.), trans. Roberta Finlayson Samsour (Prague, 1954), p. 142.

NOTES

3 David Beveridge, 'Dvořák's Abodes and Travels During the First Years of His Marriage (1873–77)', in Graham Melville-Mason (ed.), *Czech Music*, vol. 25 (Bramley, 2014), p. 108.

4 Edward Elgar, *Letters of a Lifetime*, Jerrold Northrop Moore (ed.) (London, 2012), p. 15.

5 *Letters and Reminiscences*, p. 86.

6 *Letters and Reminiscences*, p. 143.

7 *Letters and Reminiscences*, p. 82.

8 I am grateful to David Beveridge for generously sharing the fruits of his research about Vysoká.

9 *Letters and Reminiscences*, p. 149.

10 http://www.poetry-archive.com/d/the_american_flag.html, last accessed 15 December 2020.

11 *Letters and Reminiscences*, p. 152.

12 Willa Cather, *My Antonia* (Boston, 1918), p. 37.

13 Cather, p. 74.

14 Cather, p. 76.

15 Cather, p. 92.

16 *Letters and Reminiscences*, p. 150.

17 Quoted in Daniel Immerwahr, *How to Hide an Empire* (New York, 2019), p. 62.

18 *Letters and Reminiscences*, p. 151.

19 Quoted in John C. Tibbetts (ed.), *Dvořák in America, 1892–1895* (Portland, OR, 1993), p. 356.

20 Michael Beckerman, *New Worlds of Dvořák* (New York, 2003), pp. 99–110.

21 http://www.antonin-dvorak.cz/en/vysoka, last accessed 15 December 2020.

22 *Letters and Reminiscences*, p. 155.

23 *Letters and Reminiscences*, p. 158.

24 Quoted in Miraslav Ivanov, *In Dvořák's Footsteps: Musical Journeys in the New World*, Leon Karel (ed.), trans. Stania Slahor (Kirksville, MO, 1995), pp. 220–1.

25 *Letters and Reminiscences*, p. 160.

26 Quoted in Tibbetts, p. 89.

27 *Letters and Reminiscences*, p. 166.

28 Tully Potter, https://www.oxfordmusiconline.com/grovemusic/view/10.1093/gmo/9781561592630.001.0001/omo-9781561592630-e-0000044216, last accessed 19 October 2020.

NOTES

29 *Letters and Reminiscences*, pp. 165–6.
30 https://en.m.wikipedia.org/wiki/Nobody_Knows_the_Trouble_I%27ve_Seen, last accessed 2 May 2020.
31 https://imslp.org/wiki/The_Spectre's_Bride%2C_Op.69_(Dvo%C5%99%C3%A1k%2C_Anton%C3%ADn), last accessed 15 December 2020.·
32 I am grateful to Steven Bruns for this suggestion.
33 Quoted in Beckerman, p. 120.
34 Quoted in Tibbetts, p. 384.
35 Quoted in Ivanov, p. 348.
36 Otakar Dvořák, *Antonín Dvořák, My Father*, Paul J. Polansky (ed.), trans. Miroslav Nêmec (Spillville, IA, 1993), p. 36.
37 *Letters and Reminiscences*, p. 187.
38 Otakar Dvořák, p. 37.
39 https://imslp.org/wiki/4_Lieder%2C_Op.82_(Dvo%C5%99%C3%A1k%2C_Anton%C3%ADn), last accessed 15 December 2020.
40 *Letters and Reminiscences*, pp. 184–5.
41 Otakar Dvořák, p. 68.

TURNING THE PAGE

1 https://www.nytimes.com/1991/03/07/opinion/dvorak-doesn-t-live-here-anymore.html, 7 March 1991, last accessed 15 December 2020.

BARTÓK'S *LONTANO*

1 Béla Bartók, *Letters*, collected, selected, edited and annotated by János Demény, trans. Péter Balabán and István Farkas, trans. revised by Elisabeth West and Colin Mason (Budapest, 1971), p. 6.
2 Béla Bartók, *Essays*, Benjamin Suchoff (ed.), (London, 1976), p. 409.
3 *Letters*, p. 72.
4 *Essays*, p. 410.
5 *Essays*, p.10.
6 P. Ovidius Naso, *Metamorphoses*, trans. Arthur Golding (Boston, 1922), Perseus Digital Library, http://data.perseus.org/citations/urn:cts:latinLit:phi0959.phi006.perseus-eng1:10.1-10.85, last accessed 1 August 2021.

7 http://www.turkishmusicportal.org/en/types-of-turkish-music/collections-turkish-folk-music-bartok-in-turkey, last accessed 15 December 2020.
8 *Letters*, pp. 267–9.
9 *Letters*, p. 278.
10 *Letters*, p. 284.
11 *Letters*, pp. 291–3.
12 *Letters*, p. 301.
13 *Letters*, p. 331.
14 See Carl Leafstedt, 'Asheville, Winter of 1943–44: Bela Bartók and North Carolina', in *Musical Quarterly*, vol. 87, no. 2 (Oxford, 2004), pp. 219–58.
15 *Essays*, p. 408.
16 *Letters*, p. 330.
17 *Letters*, p. 307.
18 https://timesmachine.nytimes.com/timesmachine/1941/01/21/85287909.html?pageNumber=18, last accessed 4 January 2021.
19 *Letters*, p. 29.
20 *Letters*, p. 201.
21 *Essays*, pp. 29–30.
22 *Letters*, pp. 281–2.
23 See, for example, William Dusinberre, *Them Dark Days* (Oxford, 1996).

WHERE BRITTEN BELONGS?

1 Benjamin Britten, *On Receiving the First Aspen Award* (London, 1964), p. 20.
2 Elizabeth Sprague Coolidge to Nicolas Moldovan, 20 January 1941, quoted in Cyrilla Barr, *Elizabeth Sprague Coolidge: American Patron of Music* (New York, 1998), pp. 284–5.
3 Benjamin Britten, *Letters from a Life: Selected Letters and Diaries of Benjamin Britten*, Donald Mitchell and Philip Reed (eds), vol. 2: *1939–1945*, (London, 1991), p. 631.
4 See Paul Kildea, *Benjamin Britten: A Life in the Twentieth Century* (London, 2013), p. 149.
5 *Letters from a Life*, p. 633.
6 *Letters from a Life*, p. 634.
7 Quoted in Kildea, p. 147. 'Back to Britain with Britten',

Britten interviewed by Charles Reid, in *High Fidelity Magazine* (December 1959).

8 *Letters from a Life*, p. 714.
9 *Letters from a Life*, p. 749.
10 *Letters from a Life*, p. 754.
11 *Letters from a Life*, p. 715.
12 *Letters from a Life*, p. 847.
13 *Letters from a Life*, p. 911.
14 *Letters from a Life*, p. 962.
15 *Los Angeles Times*, 22 September 1941. The complete article is in *Letters from a Life*, p. 983.
16 *Letters from a Life*, p. 961.
17 *On Receiving the First Aspen Award*, p. 21.
18 John Tyrrell, 'Forster, Crabbe and Britten: The Listener, 29 May 1941', https://john-tyrrell.blogspot.com/2014/09/forster-crabbe-and-britten.html, last accessed 16 December 2020.
19 *On Receiving the First Aspen Award*, p. 22.

A CHORUS OF BIRDS

1 Quoted in *Letters from a Life*, Philip Reed, Mervyn Cooke (eds), vol. 6, *1966–1976* (Woodbridge, 2012), p. 695.
2 An earlier passacaglia in *Peter Grimes* is one of several in Britten's works related to the subject of death, in this case seeming to portray Grimes's unravelling mental state – an interlude that precedes the death of his second apprentice.
3 See Colin Matthews, 'Working Notes', in Alan Blyth, *Remembering Britten* (London, 1981), p. 178.
4 Quoted in *Letters from a Life*, p. 696.
5 Juliet Dusinberre, *Alice to the Lighthouse: Children's Books and Radical Experiments in Art* (London, 1987), p. 214.
6 Kenneth Grahame, *The Wind in the Willows* (Oxford, 1908), p. 258.

Index

Definite articles ('The', 'Les') at the beginning of titles of works are ignored for the purpose of alphabetisation. Page numbers in *italics* relate to photographs. Abbreviation: ED = Edward Dusinberre.

INDEX

INDEX

229

INDEX

Mondaytown (ED's grandparents' cottage) 8–11, 17, 27–8, 44–6
Müller-Widmann, Annie 128
Music Academy of the West 101
Muzsikás ensemble 111–12, 121
My Antonia (Cather) 62–4, 66, 80, 82, 84–5

National Conservatory of Music of America: concerts 65, 69; diversity of students and faculty 67, 68–9; Dvořák's contracts with 57, 59, 86–7; Dvořák resigns from 90–1 *see also* Thurber, Jeannette Meyer
Native Americans, 19th century attitudes towards 65–6
'New World' Symphony (no. 9) (Dvořák) 69–70, 84–5, 95
Night Mail (GPO documentary with W. H. Auden and Britten) 169, 191
Nissel, Siegmund 75, 195
Novák, Matej 87
Novotný, V. J., 'Songs of the American Indian' (article) 66

O'Neill, Richard *210*; early life and family 192, 206; joins Takács Quartet 100–3, 106, 193; musical interpretations and insights 102–3, 195, 202, 209; playing style 101–2 *see also* Takács Quartet
organ, donated and played by Dvořák 87–8
Ormai, Gábor 103–4, *105 see also* Takács Quartet
Othello (Dvořák) 65
Ovid, *Metamorphoses* 122–3

Pásztory-Bartók, Ditta (Béla Bartók's second wife) 127, 129–32, 141–2, 143, 151, 160
Pears, Peter: travels to America with Britten 166–7, 170; begins relationship with Britten 170; stays with Mayer family in Long

Island 171, 172, 173, 175–6; stays in shared house in Brooklyn 176–7; stays with Rae Robertson and Ethel Bartlett in Escondido 177, 179–84; returns to England with Britten 188; sings title role in Britten's *Peter Grimes* 188; home at Crag House, Aldeburgh 189; founds Aldeburgh Music Club 189, *190*; retreat at Horham 200; home at The Red House, Aldeburgh 198, 200
Peter Grimes (opera) (Britten) 186, 187, 188–9
'Peter Grimes' (poem) (Crabbe) 186–7
Philadelphia String Quartet 192
pianos: of Bartók 127, 129, 151; of Dvořák 58, 64; of ED's grandfather 10, 11, 43, 46, 47; of Elgar 30, 32
pigeons, Dvořák's interest in 59, 70, 86, 91–2, *91 see also* birds and birdsong
Plantation Dances (Arnold) 69
Pokorny, Jan Hird 95
Pomp and Circumstance ('Land of Hope and Glory') (Elgar) 30, 32, 44
Potter Mary 198
Potter, Tully 76

recapitulation (compositional technique): Bartók's use of 6–7, 117–18, 138–9, 140, 156–7; Dvořák's use of 96; Elgar's use of 14, 43–4 *see also* ABA form
Reed, Billy 22, 26, 32–4, 40–1; *Elgar as I Knew Him* 32–3
Rhodes, Harumi: early life and family 206; works with Richard O'Neill before Takács Quartet 101; joins Takács Quartet 75; musical interpretations and insights 79–80, 81, 97, 155, 196, 209; playing style 101–2, 157; visits Bartók Memorial House with ED 148–53;

231

INDEX